THE ULTIMATE
F·R·I·E·N·D·S
COMPANION

THE ULTIMATE

F·R·I·E·N·D·S

COMPANION

THE ONE WITH THE FIRST FIVE SEASONS

PENNY STALLINGS

WARNER WORLDWIDE PUBLISHING

This edition printed for The Book People 1999
Hall Wood Avenue
Haydock
St Helens
WA119UL

www.macmillan.co.uk

Associated companies throughout the world

ISBN 0 7522 1726 7

Designed by Blackjacks, London
Printed by New InterLitho, Italy

Acknowledgements

Kevin S. Bright, Marta Kauffman, David Crane, Jamie O'Connor, Skye Van Raalte-Herzog, Aimee Chaille, Emma Marriott, Jonathan Baker,
Colleen Mahan, Todd Stevens, Debra McGuire, Mary Rodriguez, Danna Fleishman, Phil Gonzales, Dan O'Gorman, John Eakin, Alexa Junge,
Michael Curtis, Gregory S. Malins, Michael Borkow, Adam Chase, Michael Lembeck, John Shaffner, James Burrows, Greg Grande, Sheila Kovar,
Lee Kernis, Maggie Wheeler, Elliott Gould, Jennifer Saunders, Tom Conti, Barry Secunda, Valencia Smith, Jake Melville, Charlie Carman,
Adrienne Turner, Adrian Sington, Richard Geffen, Michael Harkavy, Karen Bailey, Siobhan Williamson, Mariana Villacres

Magazine Acknowledgements

Cosmopolitan, Courtesy of Cosmopolitan Magazine; *Cowboys & Indians Magazine*, Courtesy of Cowboys & Indians Magazine;
Entertainment Weekly, Courtesy of Entertainment Weekly; *FHM*, Courtesy of FHM – FOR HIM MAGAZINE; *Good Housekeeping*,
Courtesy of Good Housekeeping; *Hello!*, Courtesy of Hello Magazine; *In Style*, Courtesy of IN STYLE Magazine; *Jane*, Courtesy of Jane Magazine;
Marie Claire, Courtesy of Marie Claire Magazine; *Men's Fitness*, Men's Fitness Magazine; *Parade*, Courtesy of Parade Publications/Gwendolen
Cates/CPI; *People Weekly*, Courtesy of PEOPLE Magazine; *Philadelphia*, Courtesy of Philadelphia Magazine/E.J. Camp; *Rolling Stone*, Courtesy of
Wenner Media, Incorporated; *seventeen*, Courtesy of seventeen magazine/Grey Zisser; *SKY TV Guide*, Courtesy of Redwood Publishing, London;
Télé Cable Satellite Hebdo, Courtesy of François Viut, Chief Editor of Télé Cable Satellite Hebdo; *TV Guide*, Courtesy of the
TV Guide Magazine Group, Inc.; *Total TV*, Courtesy of TV Guide (all rights reserved); *Us*, Courtesy of Wenner Media, Incorporated;
Who Weekly (Australia), Courtesy of WHO WEEKLY

BAFTA Award – The British Academy Award is based on a design by Mitzi Cunliffe. Used with permission from the
British Academy of Film and Television Arts; MISTER BOFFO cartoon, Courtesy of Universal Press Syndicate;
George Lucas letter dated October 4, 1996, Courtesy of George Lucas and Lucasfilm Ltd. All rights reserved;
Friends sheet music reprinted by permission. © 1995 Reprise Records.

Photography Credits

Byron J. Cohen, Bonnie Colodzin, Danny Feld, Robert Isenberg, Craig T. Mathew, Jamie O'Connor, Oliver Upton, Joseph Viles

CONTENTS

INTRODUCTION
FIVE YEARS OF FRIENDS

Have you heard the one about the sitcom that just kept getting better and better the longer it was on the air? Impossible you say? Everybody knows that it just doesn't work that way. Hit shows have a way of burning out. The pressure and the competition leads to fussing and feuding. The writers run out of steam. The stars leave to do movies and never come back. Shit happens. With one notable exception.

Friends. It had always been a solid hit, but in its fifth season it became the most-watched situation comedy in the world. And this time around, it wasn't about being a pop cultural phenomenon as it was during its first – wild – year, it was about funny. It was about being elevated to the status of "classic" comedy by even the most testy TV pundits. Their encomiums were extravagant. *Friends* had been "revitalized".... it was "newly inspired". Blah blah blah. Of course, those of us who'd been paying attention for the previous four years knew that *Friends* had always been, well, perfect – from the minute runaway bride Rachel Green stumbled into Central Perk to the last few seconds of episode 122 when she and Ross stumbled out of a Las Vegas wedding chapel.

So what are the chances of keeping a series concept so symmetrical, so compelling and so vibrant for such a long period of time? In Hollywood, people who toil in the television industry like to say that the odds of simply getting a sitcom on the air are about the same as winning the lottery. Forget about actually scoring a hit. But with *Friends* everything fell into place long before the first stale doughnut appeared on the crafts services table. "There was something about this piece that wrote itself," *Friends* co-creator Marta

Kauffman says. "It was blessed, you know. The stars were aligned." Sure enough, the show was white-hot the minute it was beamed over the airwaves. The critics swooned over its hip sensibility, its intelligence. The six cast members became overnight sensations. Even its theme song became a hit. Things were going so well that something had to go wrong. Did somebody say backlash?

Hardly anyone remembers exactly what gave rise to the whole weird situation nowadays. It might've been a reaction to a certain comely hairstyle that was slavishly imitated by thousands of female fans. Or the way the cast members' faces were suddenly plastered all over the U.S. tabloids. But mostly media turnaround was toxic fallout from a promotion where one of the Friends chugged a Diet Coke during an episode. "The Coke commercial broke the fourth wall for the show," observes executive producer Kevin S. Bright. "The characters all-of-a-sudden became commercial icons rather than something that was exclusive to the world of television." Put another way, the show's special magic had seeped so deeply into the public's collective right brains that when the cast engaged in something as secular as a commercial tie-in, it sort of, well, broke the spell. Anyway, that's one explanation.

Whatever brought it on, the whole disagreeable interlude shocked the show's young actors. Even today, five years later, you rarely read an interview with one of them wherein they don't allude to the "backlash of publicity" that came down during the show's first year. But thankfully it proved to be little more than a hiccup in the overall life of the show – due in no small part to the deft way it was handled by

I'LL BE THERE FOR YOU
By The Rembrandts

So no one told you life was gonna be this way [four claps]
Your job's a joke, you're broke, your love life's D.O.A.
It's like you're always stuck in second gear
When it hasn't been your day, your week, your month, or even your year, but

CHORUS
I'll be there for you
(When the rain starts to pour)
I'll be there for you
(Like I've been there before)
I'll be there for you
('Cause you're there for me too)

You're still in bed at ten and work began at eight
You've burned your breakfast so far, things are going great
Your mother warned you there'd be days like these
But she didn't tell when the world has brought you down to your knees

CHORUS

No one could ever know me, no one could ever see me
Seems you're the only one who knows what it's like to be me
Someone to face the day with, make it through all the rest with
Someone I'll always laugh with
Even at my worst, I'm best with you
Yeah!

the cast and the producers. Instead of trying to wage a PR war in the press, they did their jobs. They turned inward and got closer. They became *real* friends.

No matter what controversy or commotion swirled around *Friends*, it always had awesome ratings to keep it warm. Another perennial wellspring of support lay in the show's gung-ho studio audiences. These weren't just mind-numbed tourists being shuttled into the Studio 24 bleachers from bus tours as is true with so many other television shows. These were ardent fans who wrote and called and waited and pleaded to get tickets for months in advance. Once they made it in, they were so wired that the studio fairly vibrated with their excitement. "It's like you have six Ricky Martins out there that the audience is passionate to see," observes legendary television director James Burrows, "and there's this kind of wild adoration that I don't think I've seen on any other sitcom." Proof of their loyalty can be seen in the way they support the cast on a typical night's shoot. An episode of *Friends* might take three, or four, or six hours to shoot, but the studio audiences stay glued to their seats – watching intently as the writers feed the actors replacement lines, laughing at jokes they've heard again and again, crying at the sad parts, and giving the cast a thunderous ovation after the incredibly complicated process has at last come to a close.

Now that the show has gone into syndication, viewers are more caught up in the *Friends* chronicles than ever. That might have something to do with the fact that each episode of *Friends* is an installment in an ongoing saga. The stories are relayed via a fusillade of jokes, and yet the writers manage to keep them totally believable and real.

So, how do they do it? How do the *Friends'* scripts end up so uniformly on the mark, so universal in their appeal, so consistently hilarious week after week, year after year? Obvious answer: the writers are, like geniuses. And then too, they're young enough to understand first hand what these characters are going through – and, perhaps more importantly, to work till all hours getting it right. "I understand why this is an ageist business," Marta

Kauffman says. "The people who are in their twenties can stay up all night writing."

Even so, *Friends* co-creators Marta Kauffman and David Crane downplay the notion of *Friends* as being demographically oriented. And since the show's weekly audience numbers around 30 million in the US and Britain alone, they must be right. There simply aren't that many viewers in their twenties. (Do the maths.) But if *Friends'* appeal transcends age, it's because its characters are constantly grappling with the great imponderables of life.

These twentysomethings had every right to be bewildered. They'd made their entrance into the adult world at a time when the old moral compasses of the past – church, family, community – had gone on the fritz. Their ethical sensibilities had been shaped by the pop cultural zeitgeist (*The Brady Bunch*, Watergate, etc) rather than by the book, leaving them at once cynical and naïve. Monica's spacious apartment notwithstanding, this group inhabits a downsized world with far fewer choices than there were for their parents' generation. Of course, that doesn't mean that they're not going to go at life with everything they've got.

Kauffman and Crane have often said that they wanted this show to focus on a group that still had all its life choices ahead of them ... people who were still in the process of "becoming". But that state of sustained limbo turned out to be agonizingly uncomfortable for their highly-strung creations. Career, romance ... nothing seemed to fall into place for any of them. While waiting for some sort of epiphany to enlighten them (or get them laid), they drank coffee and talked and talked (and talked some more).

In this way – and in so many more – *Friends* broke all the tried and true sitcom rules: instead of showing the characters doing something, we heard them telling each other about doing something. And instead of spinning the show around comedy licks – the licks moved the story forward. Quirky doesn't begin to describe how unorthodox *Friends* was as compared to what had gone before it.

Friends debuted early in the decade at a time we can characterize (with the benefit of hindsight) as the calm before the storm in America – in that no one was talking about Monica or Kosovo or Y2K. The country had a vigorous young president at the helm, a strong economy and a prevailingly upbeat mood. And it was time for a show that reflected the changes that had occurred on the cultural and moral landscapes of American society. Time for television characters who knew about divorce and extended families, surrogate mothers and multiple births, lesbians and Lamaze, and maybe even the Fonz. With all that in mind, why don't

we return to the beginning ... to the first official day of the *Friends* era.

It was a day like any other in Los Angeles. Or Burbank to be more site specific. It was 6pm, but the sun was still blaring down on the Warner Bros. lot – as two hundred or so people lined up outside Studio 29 to see a new show called *Friends*. If you were one of them, you might have landed there because you were showing your out-of-town relatives the sights. Or perhaps you yourself were from somewhere else – and you were doing what tourists do when they visit L.A. In any case, you would have known very little about the show you were going to see – other than the fact that it was a comedy and it had that cute girl from *Family Ties* in it.

The warm up guy (they're always guys) would fill you in on the rest. About how this show revolved around a group of six people in their twenties who all lived in New York and who had known each other since forever. And how they hung out in a coffee-house called Central Perk – which was where we would find them in the opening scene.

Monica – played by Courteney Cox (applause) – was a would-be chef.

Her brother Ross – played by David Schwimmer – was a palaeontologist who was in the process of splitting up with his wife.

Rachel – played by Jennifer Aniston – was their old friend from high school who'd taken a more traditional path with her life after graduating.

Joey – played by Matt LeBlanc – was an unemployed actor who thought he was God's gift.

Phoebe – played by Lisa Kudrow – was a New Age-y folksinger with a unique take on life.

Chandler – played by Matthew Perry – was a computer programmer who had trouble with, well, just about everything.

After being introduced to the audience for the first time, the six young cast members – most of them new faces – would take their places onstage.

Quiet on the set.

We have speed.

Action!

THE FIRST SEASON

They were just a regular group of twentysomethings. OK, maybe they were better-looking than almost anybody else in the world. And, yeah, they were bright. And funny, too. And yet, for the most part, nothing went right for these six friends. That was apparent right from **The Pilot** …

Take super-smart, super-sweet **Ross Geller**, whose wife Carol had just left him. No, not for another man … for another woman. (A first for prime-time TV). It seems that Carol was – and always had been – a lesbian. Ross blamed himself not only for losing Carol's

Monica: "Okay, everybody. Relax. This is not a date. It's just two people going out to dinner and not having sex." Chandler: "Sounds like a date to me." – Chandler says it all in the pilot

love, but also for being such a knucklehead that he didn't see the signs right from the start. (Like the way Carol drank her beer out of the bottle instead of pouring it into a glass.) Whatever. Ross was crushed. Destroyed. Annihilated. Unlike many of his contemporary twentysomethings, he *liked* being "tied down" in a marriage. Sure, his career as a palaeontologist was important to him. But not like love, not like family. Hey, he's an old-fashioned guy.

And then there was **Rachel Green**. How could

▲ *"I'm going to get one of those job things."* – Rachel

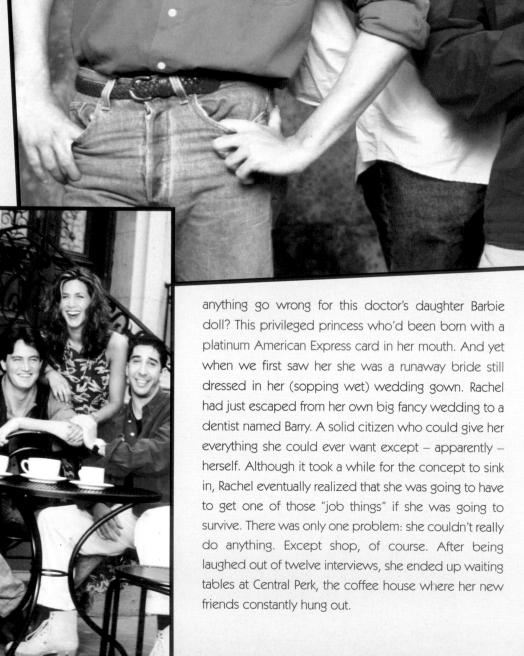

"The boys are like our brothers," says Jennifer Aniston of Matthew Perry, Matt LeBlanc and David Schwimmer. "We love our boys." ▶

It's too clean to be New York, so it must be the Warner Bros. back lot. The cast members of a new show called Friends get together for their first publicity shoot. ▼

anything go wrong for this doctor's daughter Barbie doll? This privileged princess who'd been born with a platinum American Express card in her mouth. And yet when we first saw her she was a runaway bride still dressed in her (sopping wet) wedding gown. Rachel had just escaped from her own big fancy wedding to a dentist named Barry. A solid citizen who could give her everything she could ever want except – apparently – herself. Although it took a while for the concept to sink in, Rachel eventually realized that she was going to have to get one of those "job things" if she was going to survive. There was only one problem: she couldn't really do anything. Except shop, of course. After being laughed out of twelve interviews, she ended up waiting tables at Central Perk, the coffee house where her new friends constantly hung out.

Emotional torment was a constant with **Chandler Bing**. And the pointed barbs he used to deflect the pain often boomeranged right back at his own fragile heart. In future episodes we would come to understand that his angst flowed out of his tormented childhood with his predatory mother and his recently out-of-the-closet gay father. The whole scene was a "Freudian nightmare" – just like Chandler said. And yet, it was nothing compared with the turmoil the ethereal **Phoebe Buffay** had endured in her short, twirly life.

The guitar-strumming, folk-singing Phoebe had landed in New York at the age of fourteen after her mother's suicide. Her birth-father had run out on the family when she was still an infant. And her step-father was a guest of the state prison system. She'd been on her own pretty much since forever – living in a box and playing her guitar (badly) for donations on the street. Phoebe's tumultuous history had earned her a lot of latitude with the gang. They were constantly cutting her slack – even when she blurted out a painful truth or a confidence about one of them.

Compared to Phoebe, **Joey Tribbiani** is mental health week. There doesn't seem to be a thought – let alone a care – in his Italian Stallion brain. He's cute and he knows it. Or anyway, that's the way he comes across. Of course, his true nature, as it would be revealed in future episodes, would turn out to be far more complicated.

Compulsive, neurotic, driven-to-please-others-no-matter-what-the-cost,

She's got the music in her: Phoebe started singing on the streets to stay alive after her mother committed suicide.

15

▲ "Girls at each other's throats?" observes Jennifer Aniston of the catty, business-suit-clad women on Ally McBeal. "I don't think that's real life. It exists, I'm sure, but not with us."

Monica Geller is a total wacko. She is also the person you want to have around during a crisis. She was the person who gave Rachel a place to stay when her life fell apart. And she's also the one who will make Thanksgiving dinner and homemade jam and play surrogate mum whenever someone needs help. But Monica is a pushover, as well as a sweetheart. In a scenario that will be repeated many times over the years, we will see her get suckered into bed by a whole string of losers.

We would see the Friends change considerably over their first five years of their prime-time existence. They would struggle and suffer and fight. But it's amazing how true they would stay to the characters who came to life in this first legendary episode.

~

Ross was trying to recover from the break-up of his marriage when his sensitive psyche got yet another cosmic thwack in **The One with the Sonogram (Ultrasound) at the End**. Carol, his soon-to-be ex-wife, was pregnant. But Carol hadn't come to beg him to reconcile for the sake of the baby. In fact, her lover Susan had every intention of becoming a fully-fledged parent to the baby.

Phoebe's life path had been pitted with some serious potholes. But she had a momentary reversal of fortune in **The One with the Thumb**. A mysterious deposit in her bank account was the first of several unexpected windfalls she would experience in this episode. It was followed by a detached thumb in a can of soda – which wasn't such a windfall, but the 7,000 dollars the soda company shelled out to make amends certainly was. Or it could have been if Phoebe hadn't thought it

"I grew up on The Monkees and The Beatles and was very influenced by that stuff for 'I'll Be There for You', says Michael Skloff, one of the song's composers and the husband of the show's co-creator, Marta Kauffman. According to Skloff, the models for the song were The Beatles' 'Paperback Writer' and 'I Feel Fine'. The song's story was shaped by Kauffman and Crane, and then executive producer and music maven Kevin S. Bright brought in the brilliant pop lyricist Allee Willis to tweak the lyrics. Bright also recruited the talented pop rock duo The Rembrandts to record the tune.

At a mere 45 seconds, the original version of "I'll Be There for You" was little more than a riff. But as the show began to pick up steam during the first season, disc jockeys around the country began taping the song off television and playing it on the air. Obviously, the public was ready for more — so Marta Kauffman and David Crane added additional lyrics to make it a full-blown pop anthem.

► There's nothing like a game of Twister to raise your spirits. (Especially after you've just downed a pitcher of Tiki death punch.)

▲ "It's mostly dumb-sister stuff. You know, like I mean everyone always thought of her as 'the pretty one', you know, and uh-oh, she was the first to start walking. Even though I did it later the same day. But to my parents, by then it was, like, 'Right. What else is new?'" — Phoebe on her twin sister Ursula

was bad karma to take money that wasn't really hers. Eventually she managed to unload the nasty stuff on Chandler, as a bribe to get him to stop smoking, and on Lizzie, a homeless woman she knew from her days on the street, and who called her "Weird Girl". Rachel's assets could have used a windfall. Not only had she blown off the security of marriage but somebody named FICA kept taking a huge bite out of her already meagre pay cheque.

The difference between the old and new Rachels was brought into stark relief (in **The One with George Stephanopoulos**) when a gaggle of her vacuous, rich

"I have a history with Lisa Kudrow," says director James Burrows. "She was on the *Frasier* pilot, but that role wasn't right for her. She was great, but you needed a tough producer to push Kelsey around. I was so relieved when she got *Friends*, because the role was so perfect for her. I'm sure Lisa will tell you that any time an actor is let go it's tough, but in this case it all worked out for the best."

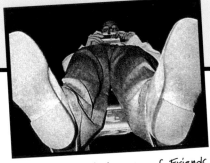

During the first season of Friends, Seventeen magazine gave the cast disposable cameras so they could photograph each other. Some attempts came out better than others — as this unusual portrait of Matthew Perry by Matt LeBlanc makes clear.

women friends from the Island showed up at Central Perk to try and lure her home. Later that night, Rachel settled in for an impromptu slumber party with Monica and Phoebe. They traded confessions over Tiki death punch and munched the wrong pizza. (Apparently theirs had mistakenly been delivered to cute political-pundit guy, George Stephanopoulos, who lived across the street.)

Meanwhile, Ross was deeply despondent over his impending anniversary with Carol. Not the anniversary of their marriage, but of the consummation of their sexual relationship. Actually, this date was even more significant than that, he told Chandler and Joey, since Carol had been his first and only lover. The guys tried to cheer him up by taking him to a hockey game. But a runaway hockey puck smashed him in the face and sent him to a hospital emergency room for the rest of the night ...

Ross's nose was back where it was supposed to be the following week in **The One with the East German Laundry Detergent**, but it was almost as painful to

◄ Monica tried to convince Rachel that she should feel great about herself for being gutsy enough to forego the security of marriage to do her own "amazing independent thing".

Like he wasn't already depressed enough: Ross ended up in a hospital emergency room after a runaway hockey puck smashed him in the face during a Rangers game. ▼

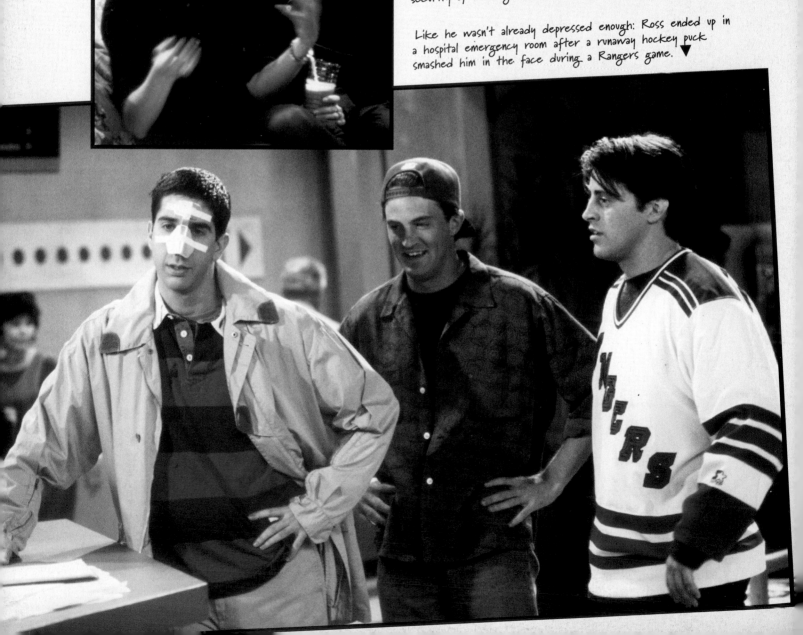

SET DESIGN

"Monica had found all the objects in her apartment at flea markets or on the street. However, if we'd known that she was going to turn into such a neat freak in future episodes, I don't think set decorator Greg Grande and I would have gone quite so eclectic with the furnishings."
– John Shaffner, art director.

"We were criticized a lot the first season," says John Shaffner, "because some people thought you couldn't get an apartment the size of Monica's in New York City. But the idea was that Monica's place was originally a larger apartment that had been chopped in half – which they did all the time in New York in the Sixties. The apartment itself was supposed to have been Monica's grandmother's which she had got a sublease on, after which her grandmother died." But in The One with the Ballroom Dancing, the building super, Mr Treeger, tells Joey that, according to the Rent Stabilization Law of 1968, Monica is subletting her apartment illegally. Apparently Mr Treeger hadn't talked to John Shaffner.

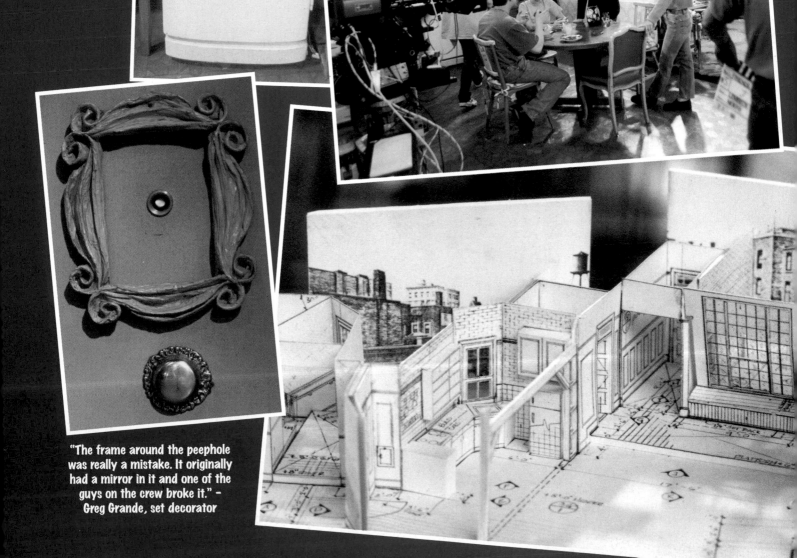

"The frame around the peephole was really a mistake. It originally had a mirror in it and one of the guys on the crew broke it." – Greg Grande, set decorator

watch him trying to confess his feelings to Rachel during their semi-date at the laundromat.

Determined to disprove Joey's prediction that he and Rachel were "never gonna happen", Ross joined Rachel on the balcony (in **The One with the Blackout**) to tell her how he felt. And then – out of nowhere – a manic cat leaped on his back, throwing him into a state of hysteria. As he spun around, struggling to get the cat off his shoulders, the gang remained oblivious to what was going on outside the window and joined in together for a rousing sing-along of "Top of the World". Later Rachel and Phoebe went on a search for the cat's owner, and discovered to their delight (and Ross's dismay) that it belonged to a new arrival in the neighbourhood – the studly Paolo, a handsome Italian guy who barely spoke English.

In only seven episodes, the Friends had grappled with love, blackouts and lesbians, and now it was time for them to face up to death, as they got the sad news that Nana, Ross and Monica's beloved grandmother, was on her way out. Monica and Ross rushed to the hospital (in **The One Where Nana Dies Twice**), where their mother took a break from her grief to give Monica a hard time about her hair. "Relax," Ross advised his sister as she started to lose it. "We're going to be here for a while, and we still have 'boyfriends' and your 'career' to cover."

Monica needed all the support she could get – especially during the

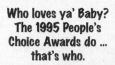

Who loves ya' Baby? The 1995 People's Choice Awards do ... that's who.

The guys contemplate the fate of Marcel the Monkey after getting the sad news that their little pal has reached sexual maturity and has got to move on to a place where he can get some "hot monkey lovin'."

her. And for the umpteenth time, she ignored him.

Thanksgiving was fast approaching and this year Ross would have something to give thanks for when he pre-natally bonded with his baby. Leaning over Carol's belly, he sang "Hey, hey, I'm your daddy … I'm the one without any breasts" to the tune of The Monkees' theme song.

In **The One Where Underdog Gets Away**, Rachel was feeling deprived because she couldn't raise the money to go to Vail with her family for their annual Thanksgiving ski trip – until the gang chipped in to buy her a ticket. And Chandler was in one of his moods, because Thanksgiving was the infamous day on which his parents had told him they were getting divorced. But at least everyone was together, and Monica was

brief, bizarre moment in Nana's hospital room when the old lady temporarily revived while she and Ross were saying good-bye to (what they thought was) her dead body. "This almost never happens," Nana's nurse assured them. Later, at his mother's behest, Ross braved the wilds of Nana's closet to find just the right shoes for her farewell appearance. Like the good boy he was, Ross had done everything right on this melancholy day – until he fell into an open grave at the cemetery. Later, while ga-ga on painkillers, he told Rachel for the umpteenth time that he loved

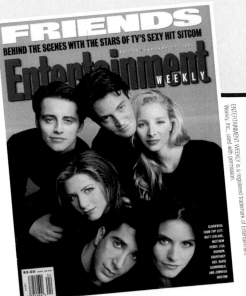

27 January 1995
The cast of Friends was still new enough on the scene, when Entertainment Weekly did this cover story in 1995, for their names to be listed alongside their photos.

cooking them a turkey. And there was excitement aplenty when the gigantic Underdog float broke free from the Macy's parade and went floating over the city. But when they all rushed out on the roof to check out the bizarre sight, they got locked out of the building. By the time they made it back to the apartment, their Thanksgiving feast had been burned to a crisp – and Rachel had missed her flight.

Before you could say hiatus, the gang was back and confronting the holi-day blues again (in **The One with the Monkey**). This time it was New Year's Eve – and everyone was concerned about who they would be with at their annual party. They decided that it would take a little of the pressure off if they all made a pact to stay dateless, but then Phoebe met a cute physicist named Max and backed out of the agreement. Then Chandler sheep-ishly admitted that he'd invited Janice, and Monica had decided she wanted to bring her old boyfriend, Fun Bobby. Rachel had asked Paolo, and Joey had invited Sandy, a hot girl from work. That left only Ross without someone to be with. But by then he was forging a relationship with a spunky little monkey named Marcel that a friend had rescued from a lab. Hardly anything went right for the gang with their dates that night. By the time the night was over, it turned out that their New Year's Eve no-date pact had worked out after all.

> "We figured out pretty early on that the comedy of *Friends* is really just about very universal emotional situations. It's about falling in love, finding a job, dealing with parents, death, birth, monkeys and lesbians". - David Crane

The gang got a chance to see for themselves what havoc Chandler's mother could wreak when she paid him a visit in **The One with Mrs Bing**. Nora Tyler (her *nom de plume*) was on a national tour to publicize her latest throbbing romance novel on the TV talk shows, and Chandler was mortified by her naughty banter with Jay Leno on *The Tonight Show*. Then there was Nora and Ross. Not that their encounter was all *that* wicked. It was just a kiss. (OK, a sexy kiss.) She was just trying to pump up Ross's ego after watching it deflate as he watched Rachel and Paolo flirt over dinner. Joey caught them in the act and accused Ross of breaking The Code. Ross confessed his crime to Chandler – who eventually forgave him.

Ross was so jealous of Paolo that when Rachel announced they were heading off for a romantic week-end in a Poconos bungalow (in **The One with the**

> "Look, just because you played tonsil tennis with my mom doesn't mean you know her." - Chandler

Dozen Lasagnas), he even considered turning him in to Immigration. The couple was even more annoyingly lovey-dovey – until Phoebe told Rachel that Paolo had put the make on her. Ciao, Paolo. Seeing an opening, Ross tried to console her, but Rachel told him she had had it with guys. Then, just for good measure, she thoughtlessly blurted out the sex of his child (a boy).

While none of the Friends had made a move on each other thus far in the series, they did get more intimate in **The One with the Boobies**. Chandler wandered into the girls' place and accidentally happened upon Rachel getting out of the shower. Rachel covered herself with an afghan, but Chandler could still see her "nippular areas". For days afterwards, Chandler couldn't stop staring at Rachel's breasts, even though they were (of course) covered. So Rachel took it upon herself to even the score. She snuck into the guy's shower to see Chandler's "pee-pee", but ended up seeing Joey's privates instead. Naturally, Joey was then obligated to catch Rachel in the shower, but – surprise – he got Monica. Later that day Monica went over to turn the tables on Joey in the shower and instead found his wet, naked father all lathered up – and really happy to see her.

▲ Monica was thrilled when Phoebe got her an audition with a client who was opening a new restaurant. She whipped up all of her most sophisticated dishes, but the guy (guest star Jon Lovitz) showed up stoned out-of-his-mind with a bad case of the munchies. This was the closest Monica had come to getting someone to take her seriously as a chef – and it was a total disaster.

"When we started out," recalls Kevin S. Bright, "we were media darlings. We were labelled as something you hadn't seen on television, something new and fresh. But all that media attention and the show's incredible popularity brought on a backlash. And it was, like, 'Hey, enough already. I don't want to see those actors on another magazine cover. I don't want to see any more merchandising. Enough with that show. It's too in my face!"

21 July 1997
The cover of this Swiss magazine lured readers with a headline announcing an interview with Courteney Cox and Matthew Perry wherein they would explain why "Friends was finished". Problem was that Friends wasn't finished and neither star had been interviewed. Oh yeah, and the cover photos were about three years out-of-date.

Courtesy of François Viot, Chief Editor of Télé Cable Satellite Hebdo

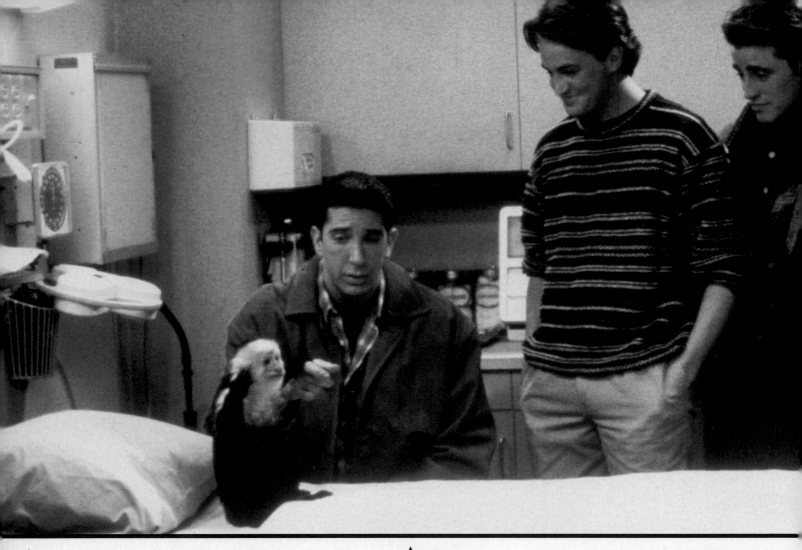

There were no boobies or naked Italian guys in **The One with the Candy Hearts**. Just romantic frustration – because it was Valentine's Day and Cupid was hell-bent on having the last laugh. Things got off to a rotten start when Chandler agreed to go out on a blind date that Joey had got him.

Just his luck: the date turned out to be Janice – whom he'd already dumped twice in the past five months.

For their Valentine's Day therapy, the girls talked about creepy boyfriends past, and decided to expel them from their psyches with a cleansing ritual – a boyfriend bonfire. Standing around a smouldering trash can, the three women threw piles of old boyfriend memorabilia into the flames. Then Rachel spritzed the fire with Paolo's grappa and the whole mess exploded into a mini-inferno.

And finally, Ross went out to dinner with Kristen, his first date since the divorce, only to be seated next to Carol and Susan. When Susan got called away, Ross

▲

Phoebe: "How's he doing?"
Ross: "The doctor got the K out and an O."
Chandler: "We think he was trying to spell monkey."
— The concerned gang gathered at the Emergency Room after Marcel swallowed several Scrabble tiles in The One with Two Parts

invited Carol to join them and then proceeded to ignore his date and talk only to her. Not surprisingly, Kristen took a pass and left Ross with his ex. Would she consider giving their relationship another shot, he ventured? Not a chance, she said, but they shared a kiss and it was clear that there was still a deep bond between them.

Career prospects began to pick up for both Monica and Chandler in **The One with the Stoned Guy**. Monica got an audition with a client of Phoebe who was opening a new restaurant. After cooking all day, Monica was dismayed to see that the guy was stoned, and he had a bad case of the munchies. He tried to eat everything in sight … particularly sweets. This was the closest Monica had come to getting someone to take her seriously as a chef – and it was a disaster. She had no career, and no life. Other than that things couldn't have been better.

Chandler, a devout career temp, got an unsolicited promotion to processing supervisor from his boss,

▲ Ross: "I figured that after work I'd pick up a bottle of wine, go over there and try to ... woo her." Chandler: "Hey, you know what you should do? Take her back to the 1890s when that phrase was last used."

Meanwhile, Joey started dating Ursula, Phoebe's twin sister. Ross started attending Lamaze class with Carol and Susan, and Monica and Rachel took up with two very cute doctors (guest stars George Clooney and Noah Wylie). They met in the Emergency Room, where Rachel landed after her accident with the Christmas lights (she was only trying to take them down).

The best way for Ross to express his feelings to Rachel (in **The One with the Poker**) was to let her win at poker. She needed some strokes: not only had she blown a job interview at Saks, she'd just found out that Barry and her best friend Mindy were engaged (in **The One Where the Monkey Gets Away**). Never mind that she had lost Ross's beloved monkey Marcel, while monkey-sitting for him. And that she had got Ross in trouble for keeping an exotic animal in captivity by reporting the disappearance to Animal Control. And that the Animal Control Officer just happened to be someone who knew her from high school and hated her guts. Thank goodness for Rachel's downstairs neighbour, Mr Heckles – who at least got Marcel off the streets – even if he did claim that Marcel was his pet. Anyone else would have had it up to here, but Ross was in the midst of trying to connect with Rachel later that night when Barry suddenly barged in to tell her that he couldn't go through with the wedding to Mindy – because he was still in love with her. Unfortunately (in **The One with the Evil Orthodontist**) Rachel, while intending to break things off with Barry, ended up making hot-monkey-love in his dental chair.

Rachel's next surprise was a call from Mindy, who wanted her to be a maid of honour at their wedding.

▲ "Look, I know he's not perfect. But the truth is ... at ... the end of the day, I still really want to be Mrs Dr Barry Farber, DDS." Mindy ends up forgiving the Evil Orthodontist.

"Big" Al Kostelic. Anyone else would have been thrilled, but Chandler was conflicted. Sure, he liked the money part and the office with the window, but he didn't want to worry about his WENUS (Weekly Estimated Net Usage System).

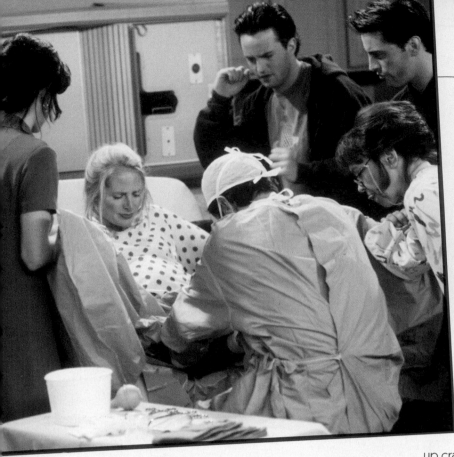

ENTERTAINMENT WEEKLY is a registered trademark of Entertainment Weekly, Inc. used with permission.

◄ Carol said that trying to push the baby out of her body was like trying to push a pot roast through her nostril. (By the way, Ross and Susan didn't make it in time for all of Carol's labour because they were still locked in the janitor's closet.)

to Barry's office to confront him together. Rachel stuck with the programme – blasting Barry and cutting him loose – but Mindy held back. Whatever his faults, it was worth it to Mindy to be Mrs Dr Barry Farber, DDS.

In **The One with the Ick Factor**, Rachel had a very sexy dream (complete with moaning and murmuring) that obviously involved Ross – and, as luck would have it, he happened to be watching. He was so thrilled that he did a little dance for joy and ended up crashing into the table – which woke Rachel from her reverie. But she was still deep into her dream and the air was thick with possibility – until Ross's pager began to beep. His baby was coming. Right now.

The whole gang gathered excitedly at the hospital (in **The One with the Birth**). Of course, things were still plenty dicey between Ross and Susan – even though they'd done a bit of bonding in Lamaze class. Still, they couldn't stop taking potshots at each other, even after Carol started having contractions. "I'm trying to get a person out of my body," Carol yelled, "and you're not making it any easier!" With that, she threw them both out. They continued to bicker in the hallway, each blaming the other for upsetting Carol. Finally Phoebe forced them both into a utility closet to hash things out. Naturally they got locked inside, and no amount of screaming or banging helped to attract attention. Now they were going to miss the birth, and it was all the other one's fault.

Rachel was so relieved that she immediately said yes – even though her feelings for Mindy ran the gamut from resentment to extreme guilt. It turned out that there was something else on Mindy's mind: she had a funny feeling that Barry was having an affair. Rachel quickly pooh-poohed that idea, but Barry had been weird when they were first engaged, too. Mindy thought that might have been because that was when she and Barry had started their affair. That did it for Rachel; it was time to come clean with Mindy. After Mindy recovered, they hatched a plan to get back at the Evil Orthodontist; they would go

15 September 1995 People buy magazines when she's on the cover. Courteney Cox smiles out from the cover of Entertainment Weekly.

"Carol and Susan are based on our two best friends in New York. We didn't create them for any particular political reason or because of lesbian chic. It was just an opportunity to tell a really interesting story."
– Marta Kauffman and David Crane

Fortunately both Ross and Susan made it into the delivery room in time to see little Ben come into the world. Ross said he looked like his Uncle Ed covered in Jell-O and Phoebe thought he looked exactly like Susan. (Phoebe, by the way, had to watch everything from a vent in the ceiling where she had got trapped while trying to find an escape route out of the utility closet.)

Ross's museum decided to send him to China to pick up a priceless dinosaur bone (in **The One Where Rachel Finds Out**). Just before Ross's departure, Chandler stupidly let slip to Rachel that Ross was "hopelessly in love" with her, and Rachel rushed off to the airport to propose to Ross that

they give Them a try. When she missed him, she quickly dashed off a note and gave it to the flight attendant – who promptly gave it to the wrong man.

Later, as Rachel was standing out on the balcony with a date, listening to him prattle on about how much he hated Ed Begley Jr and his stupid electric car, she had a vision of Ross – who told her that he'd loved her since the ninth grade. Then the sweet spectre kissed her passionately, and she knew immediately what she had to do. She rushed to the airport to meet him when he returned from China – only to see him deplane accompanied by another woman. End of the First Season ...

"They're tiny and chubby and so sweet to touch,
But soon they'll grow up and resent you so much.
Now they're yelling at you and you don't know why.
You cry and you cry and you cry
And you cry and you cry and you cry ... "
— Phoebe sings a cheerful new-baby song for Ross

▼

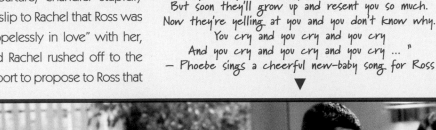

"When we started (Friends)," says Matthew Perry, "we were scared and our lives just completely changed overnight."

18 May 1995
Wanna buy five copies for my mother ... The Friends see their smiling faces on the cover of Rolling Stone.

JENNIFER ANISTON
PROFILE

When she was just sixteen years old, one of her drama teachers sat Jennifer Aniston down and warned her that she had a talent for comedy – and that it might keep her from "going deep". She assured him that she wasn't a comedienne. Boy, was she wrong.

One of the most surprising things about Jennifer is how funny she can be – looking, well, the way she does, and staying so solidly within the realistic boundaries of her character. She isn't big. She isn't loud. She doesn't make faces and stick out her tongue. In other words, she is not Jenny McCarthy. Her comedy always comes from a very controlled, modulated place. There's nothing better than seeing her (as Rachel) lose it. But even then, Jennifer Aniston is always in control.

Born in 1969 in Sherman Oaks, California, Jennifer spent a year of her childhood living in Greece. Her family then relocated to New York City. Her parents divorced when she was nine and she remained with her mother. Reacting to the divorce, Jennifer became a rebellious wise-cracker and a difficult kid. "I figured if I was bad enough, they'd have to come to the principal's office," she says. "It was me bringing them back together again."

However painful her feelings about her parents' split might have been, no emotion could compare to her passionate desire to act. As far

"David Schwimmer is the most committed, talented person,"
– Jennifer Aniston

Rachel's father, the overbearing Dr. Green, was infuriated when she abandoned her fiancé Barry on her wedding day. For what? To live in the city? Come on, she couldn't do anything – let alone support herself. He knew she'd come crawling back. She was a flake, but not a crazy flake. Her mother, on the other hand, was completely in sync with Rachel's longing to have her own life. In fact, she wanted one of her own – and she was willing to go through a messy divorce to get it. She'd spent 25 years catering to "her Barry" she told Rachel – and now it was her turn to shine. Rachel tried not to take sides in her parents' bitter break-up – although she clearly sympathized with her mother. Where her two sisters stood on the matter, we didn't know. What was the deal with those two anyway? Rachel hardly ever mentioned them – except to say that they weren't close. Was there a sisterly feud between them? Let's hope so. And let's hope that the day will come when we get to see all three of the Green sisters act out.

back as the age of twelve, Jennifer knew that she wanted to take up permanent residence in the land of make-believe. "I remember dreaming about it, about being on TV." Her resolve grew even stronger after seeing *Children of a Lesser God* on Broadway. "I was sitting in the second or third row," she recalls, "and I was just so blown away, and I walked out saying, 'That's what I want to do.'" You would think that Jennifer's family would have been all for it: her mother Nancy was an actress and model and her father is John Aniston, the long-time soap-opera actor best known as the villain Victor Kiriakis on the long-running *Days of Our Lives*. Even her godfather was a household name – her dad's good friend and fellow Greek, actor Telly Savalas of *Kojak* fame. But her father would rather have seen her do almost anything else.

Jennifer sparkles during a pause in shooting the scene where she has spent hours regaling a hapless passenger (Hugh Laurie) with the entire saga of her and Ross during the flight to London.

"Well, I wasn't terribly thrilled," he has been quoted as saying. "I don't think any father who knows anything about this business would be thrilled to have a daughter in it." What John Aniston didn't realize then was how determined his little girl was. "I wanted her to go to college, and she just didn't want to," he says. "She was anxious to get on with it. Once she decided what she wanted to do, she was very driven."

Education for Jennifer meant honing her talent. If she had to be in school, then let it be like the one in *Fame*, where she could pursue her dream. "I'd seen *Fame* I don't know how many times. I got the idea that I could go to a school for acting and get started ... the school was a lot of fun. I didn't get the parts in big plays, but I definitely enjoyed myself."

After graduating from 'Music and Art' in 1987, Jennifer continued to live at home with her mother in an apartment building on 92nd Street and Columbus Avenue. "At the time [it] was pretty seedy. But for me it was amazing. We were on the twenty-first floor with a balcony – you could see the Empire State Building. It was in, like, a project, but it was beautiful. Her days were spent auditioning and her nights waitressing at a well-known Manhattan hamburger joint. "I couldn't wait to finally go out and make my own [money]," she remembers. "The idea of never relying on someone else always thrilled me." After landing a few small parts in a couple of off-Broadway productions, she decided to move to L.A. where the real action was. "In the summer of '89 I came to visit my dad in California and started auditioning," she says, "which was the scariest thing – meeting people who asked, 'What have you done? Theatre in New York?' I hadn't done much, so everything on my resume' was made up."

Rachel found out that Joey had been using her bra as a sling to fling water balloons off the roof in The One Where Joey Moves Out.

Rachel Green had switched from the fussy designer clothes she'd financed with her father's credit card to more casual jeans and T-shirts after dumping her dentist fiancé and moving to New York. But her clothes gradually grew more sophisticated as she climbed the career ladder in the fashion world, and costume designer Debra McGuire had a blast during the fourth and fifth seasons putting her in tailored suits for work and sexy strapless dresses and strappy high heels for her evenings out.

Credits or no, Jennifer managed to find herself an agent and to land a few bit parts here and there. But she kept missing out on the bigger parts. Her agent finally suggested she change her look. She immediately noticed a difference in the way casting agents and producers regarded her. But while struggling to cover her expenses, she looks back on this period with a kind of bittersweet longing. "You always miss parts of your past," she says. "Back then it was familiar and safer, and now you have no idea what's around the corner." Around the corner turned out to be a pretty nice neighbourhood for Jennifer Aniston. There have been movies (*She's the One, Till There Was You, Picture Perfect, The Object of My Affection*) and spectacular boyfriends. And last but not least, there is *Friends* – the gig that has turned out to be the most perfect fit.

"It happened so fast," she has said of getting the show. "I went in, read the script, laughed out loud, got home and an hour later had the part." The show's producers (Kevin S. Bright, Marta Kauffman, and David Crane) knew immediately that they had found their Rachel. "We didn't see a Rachel at all until Jennifer walked in," says Marta Kauffman "Then it was amazing because there Rachel was. Jennifer just had this incredible ability to play such a brat and make you love her anyway."

And now Rachel and Ross have staged a major coup in the very last minutes of the final show – by getting married at an all-night wedding chapel in Las Vegas. Or did they? Whatever happens, it's good to know that, despite her success on the big screen, Jennifer Aniston will be there for the opening episode of the show's sixth season. "We're all with *Friends* until *Friends* dies. If one of us goes, we all go. One of us wouldn't leave. It wouldn't be the show it is without each of us."

> **"When you watch the show in reruns ... it's so funny to be flipping channels and see an old episode and think, 'God, we were awful. Such babies.'"**
> – *Jennifer Aniston*

Talk about a good sport. Jennifer Aniston went through a complete episode of *Friends* with a moustache drawn on her face.

JOEY'S BRILLIANT CAREER

No one has ever suffered more for his art than Joey Tribbiani. His first real acting job was playing the title role in an unspeakably bad musical called *Freud*. Then (in **The One with the Butt**) he got a gig in an Al Pacino movie. Unfortunately the part called for him to be Al's "butt-double" in a shower scene. And then Joey (or "Butt Guy" as the director called him) managed to get himself fired by challenging the director's interpretation of the butt's motivation in the scene.

A modelling job plastered Joey's face on giant public-service posters that went up all over the city along with the tag line, "What Mario Isn't Telling You ... You Never Know Who Might Have VD". Then, after missing out on the starring role of Santa in a department store Christmas promotion, he managed to land the much-coveted part of Santa's helper in **The One with the Monkey**. Another of Joey's odd jobs was donating sperm to a sperm bank. It didn't really require acting talent – although he did have to keep himself motivated to pull it off.

Joey's job as a perfume spritzer in a department store allowed him to get into character – kind of. He assumed the part of Hombre Man No. 2, a perfume-packing cowboy in Western drag. Joey was so into the part that he ended up in a showdown with the store's original after-shave dude, Hombre Man No. 1. But his rival got so carried away during their duel that he squirted a little old man in the eye – and that resulted in him being fired. The victorious Joey ended up walking into a cardboard sunset with a purty little gal from cosmetics.

Joey got massacred in the reviews of his next theatrical outing. "In a mediocre play," a critic wrote, "Joey Tribbiani was able to achieve new levels of sucking." This started Joey thinking that maybe it was time to pack in the

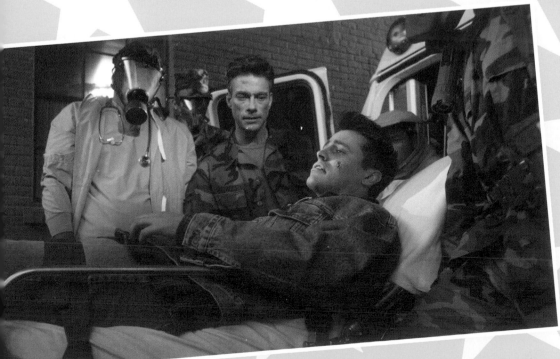

◀ Joey tries to steal the scene from Jean-Claude Van Damme.

▲ Joey's stalker Erica (guest star Brooke Shields) loved Joey's fingers so much she could bite them off.

Dear Dr Ramoray

Know that I love you and would do anything to have you.

Your not-so-secret Admirer,

Erica Ford

P.S. Enclosed please find 14 of my eyelashes!

acting thing. And he probably would have, if he hadn't got an audition for the legendary daytime soap *Days of Our Lives*. This was the break he'd been wanting for ten years! Joey became the handsome neurosurgeon, Dr Drake Ramoray, and he was actually pretty good in the role. In fact, he became so famous in the part that he had his very own stalker (in **The One with the Superbowl**). Having your privacy invaded is scary, and Joey's stalker, Erica (guest star Brooke Shields), was for sure a wack-job; but she also happened to be gorgeous. The fact that Erica couldn't seem to tell the difference between the TV and real-life Joeys got to be a little hard to manage, though. The situation came to a head when Erica came storming into Joey and Chandler's apartment in a jealous rage. Ross leaped to the rescue by telling Erica that Joey was actually Hans Ramoray, Drake's evil twin, and off she went into the night to track down the real Dr Drake.

By this point, Joey was on such a roll that he even managed to land a part in a Jean-Claude Van Damme movie. This may have been helped by the fact that he was friendly with one of the stars – Marcel the monkey, who was now an actor, too. Unfortunately, Joey was so over the top in his big dying scene that the director threw him out. But what did he care? He was rich! Yes, by **The One with the Prom Video**, he was actually starting to pull some real money on his soap – enough to be able to pay Chandler back for all the pizza he'd treated him to over the years.

Dr Drake Ramoray's life was cut short painfully in **The One Where Dr Ramoray Dies** when Joey was fired for claiming in an interview with *Soap Opera Digest* that he wrote a lot of his own lines. "Write this, Jerkweed," sneered Dr Ramoray's true creator, as he pushed Joey's character down an elevator shaft. Joey concealed the fact that the show had given him the elbow for as long as he could. A two-page-long credit-card bill (in **The One Where Eddie Won't Go**) got him back out into the grind – and fast. He went to one audition after another, but the only thing he was offered was a two-line role as a cab driver in *Another World*.

Barely able to make a dent in his debts, Joey was hurting for money so badly (in **The One with the Chicken Pox**) that Chandler offered to get him a job as an entry-level computer processor at his company. Joey couldn't imagine how he could pull off a job like that, but Chandler told him that all he had to do was to get

▲ "I don't know. When I was little, I wanted to be a veterinarian. But then I found out you had to stick your hands into cows and stuff." — Joey

into character – just as he would for a role. Joey went a bit overboard, transforming himself into the dapper Joseph, a family man with a wife named Karen and two little girls, Ashley and Brittany. In fact, he metamorphosed so thoroughly into Joseph that he covered up one of his ambitious alter ego's mistakes by blaming it on Chandler.

The choreographer of a hot, new off-Broadway show seemed to be under the impression that Joey had performed with Twyla Tharp and The American Ballet Theater. (Probably because Joey had written it on his resume so he could get into the audition.)

Oh how the mighty have fallen. It seems like only yesterday that Joey was continuing character, Dr Drake Ramoray on *Days of Our Lives,* and now he was reduced to auditioning for a two-line role as a cab driver on *Another World.*

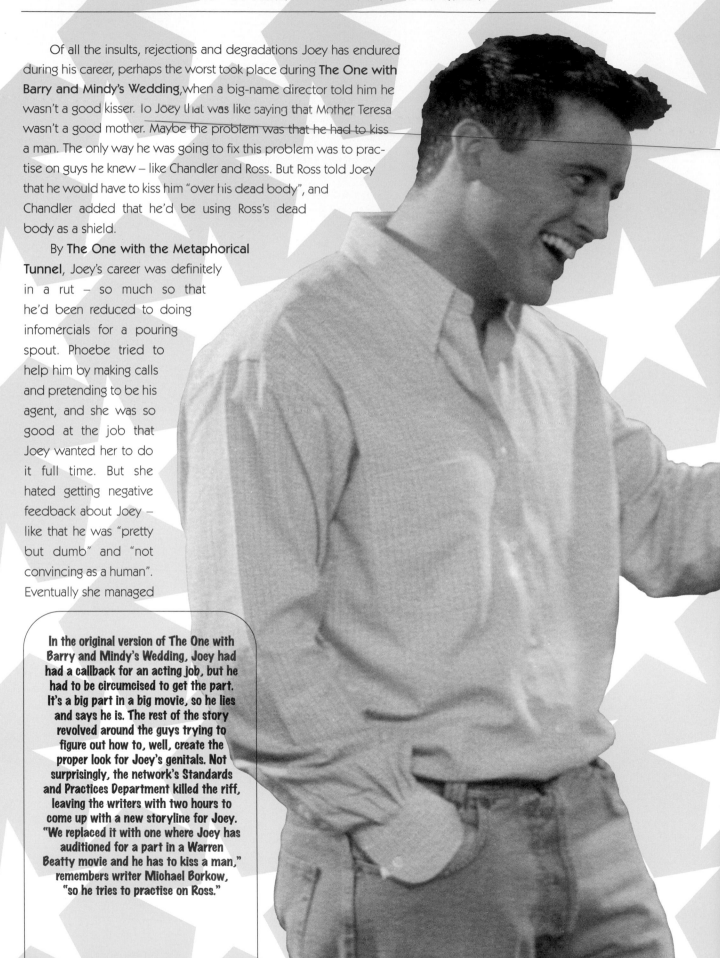

Of all the insults, rejections and degradations Joey has endured during his career, perhaps the worst took place during **The One with Barry and Mindy's Wedding,** when a big-name director told him he wasn't a good kisser. To Joey that was like saying that Mother Teresa wasn't a good mother. Maybe the problem was that he had to kiss a man. The only way he was going to fix this problem was to practise on guys he knew – like Chandler and Ross. But Ross told Joey that he would have to kiss him "over his dead body", and Chandler added that he'd be using Ross's dead body as a shield.

By **The One with the Metaphorical Tunnel**, Joey's career was definitely in a rut – so much so that he'd been reduced to doing infomercials for a pouring spout. Phoebe tried to help him by making calls and pretending to be his agent, and she was so good at the job that Joey wanted her to do it full time. But she hated getting negative feedback about Joey – like that he was "pretty but dumb" and "not convincing as a human". Eventually she managed

In the original version of *The One with Barry and Mindy's Wedding,* Joey had had a callback for an acting job, but he had to be circumcised to get the part. It's a big part in a big movie, so he lies and says he is. The rest of the story revolved around the guys trying to figure out how to, well, create the proper look for Joey's genitals. Not surprisingly, the network's Standards and Practices Department killed the riff, leaving the writers with two hours to come up with a new storyline for Joey. "We replaced it with one where Joey has auditioned for a part in a Warren Beatty movie and he has to kiss a man," remembers writer Michael Borkow, "so he tries to practise on Ross."

to convince him that he should go back to his agent Estelle.

As a back-up, Joey took a job teaching an adult education class in soap-opera acting at the Learning Connection (in **The One with the Race Car Bed**). His first piece of advice to the class was that they were "going to have to become much more attractive" if they expected ever to get a job on a soap. Next he showed them a few tricks of the trade – like how, if he had to cry, he just cut a hole in his trouser pocket and tweezed a hair from Down There. His teaching technique was a little unorthodox, but he must have been doing something right, because one of his students got a callback for a part on *All My Children*. The thing was Joey was up for the part, too. Maybe that's why, when the guy asked him for some pointers, Joey told him to play the boxer gay.

It hasn't been all misery in Joey's brilliant career. In fact, it was only a matter of weeks before he was up for a fabulous new job (in **The One with All the Jealousy**): a singing part in a musical version of *A Tale of Two Cities*. There was a problem, though, in that the role also required him to dance. "With your background," the assistant director assured him, referring to Joey's near-fictional resumé, "it'll be a piece of cake." At the callback the next day, the AD had Joey take over to demonstrate some flashy moves to the group. Naturally Joey taught them the only thing he knew. "That's the best I could get out of 'em", he told the perplexed director later, as the group did a frantic Cabbage Patch.

Joey was dazzled by Kate, his co-star in a very bad off-off Broadway play.

39

▲ "At one time or another in his career, every actor thinks he stinks," Charlton Heston told Joey after he'd tried to explain that the reason he'd sneaked into his private shower was that he stank.

It was back to a life of leisure and poverty for Joey. But at least he was in his old apartment with Chandler. Finally he got a small part in a Charlton Heston movie (in **The One with Joey's Dirty Day**). First, though, he was off on a weekend fishing trip with his old man. When he got back, he discovered to his horror that he was due on the set immediately. There wasn't even time for him to take a shower – although he hadn't had one for three days. He made it to the set on time, but he stank – and everybody on the set was aware of it. He sneaked into Charlton Heston's dressing room to use his private bathroom and, naturally, he was busted in the act. Panicked, Joey tried to explain that he was going to be working with Heston in a scene, and that he stank. Softening, Heston sat him down and told him kindly

that, at one time or another in his career, every actor thinks he stinks ...

In **The One Where Phoebe Hates PBS**, Joey's agent got him a gig hosting a PBS telethon. Or that's what he thought it was. But when he arrived on the set, the floor manager showed him to a telephone. Not only was he not the host, he wasn't even on camera. He tried to get the guy at the end of his row to trade with him, but they ended up scuffling over the seat and falling behind a table. At least the brawl was on camera.

Joey was on such a losing streak that he didn't even land the role of a 29-year-old Italian guy from Queens (in **The One with the Inappropriate Sister**). He'd been beaten out by Talia Shire, his agent told him. How could that be, he asked in disbelief: she was a woman, for crying out loud. "What can I tell you?" she shrugged. "She nailed it." Why didn't Joey just write a movie or a play that

▼ "Can you see me now?" Joey wasn't the host on the PBS Telethon like he thought. He wasn't even on camera.

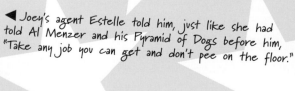

▲ Ross: "This would be the place where you explain the hat." Joey: "Oh yeah, well, there's this play, right? And I'm up for the part of this sophisticated international guy, so I figure that everyone at the audition is going to be wearing this ultra-hip, high-fashion stuff."

◄ Joey's agent Estelle told him, just like she had told Al Menzer and his Pyramid of Dogs before him, "Take any job you can get and don't pee on the floor."

he could star in, Ross suggested. "You know, like those *Good Will Hunting* guys." Ross, who was badly in need of something to do, offered to keep Joey on track with his new project. But that wasn't easy when Chandler was around to distract him with their favourite life-threatening game, Fireball. Ross reproached Chandler for keeping Joey from his art and they ended up having a major fight. When he finally did write his play, it turned out to be a fantasy wherein two characters named Ross and Chandler made up with each other and told the "handsome man" (played by Joey) how much they cared about him. His scenes for Monica and Rachel were a little more racy. So racy that they threw down the pages in disgust and told him he was sick, sick, sick.

When Joey was up for a part in a play that called for him to be "a real cool, suave international guy – a real clothes horse", Rachel offered to do a make-over on him at Bloomingdale's in **The One with Joey's Bag**. She got him looking really fine – except she wanted him to carry a rather feminine-looking

Both Joey and Ben got callbacks when they auditioned for a cereal commercial featuring a father and his small son. But they had such different looks that they'd been paired with other actors. Tensions ran high and the situation spooked Joey so much that he blew his reading. Later Ross told him he was sorry things had gone so badly, but Joey told him it wasn't his fault that he sucked. ▼

bag. He should have known something was amiss when the guys teased him about the bag so unmercifully. But, by then, Joey was in love; you could keep everything in this baby – your address book, your keys and a sandwich. At the audition, the bag attracted more attention from the producers than Joey. They asked him to read without the "purse". Once again Estelle had to tell him he hadn't got the part. This time though it wasn't his acting that sucked, it was his fashion sense.

Joey was miffed (in **The One Where Rachel Smokes**) when Ross's son Ben got an audition for a commercial from a well-known casting director – someone Joey had been trying to see for years. Ross told him they were also reading for actors to play the child's father, and why didn't he come in with them and try to get the part. Both Joey and Ben got callbacks, but that's when things started to get touchy. Joey and Ben had such different looks that they'd been paired with other actors. That meant that if one got the role, the other wouldn't. At

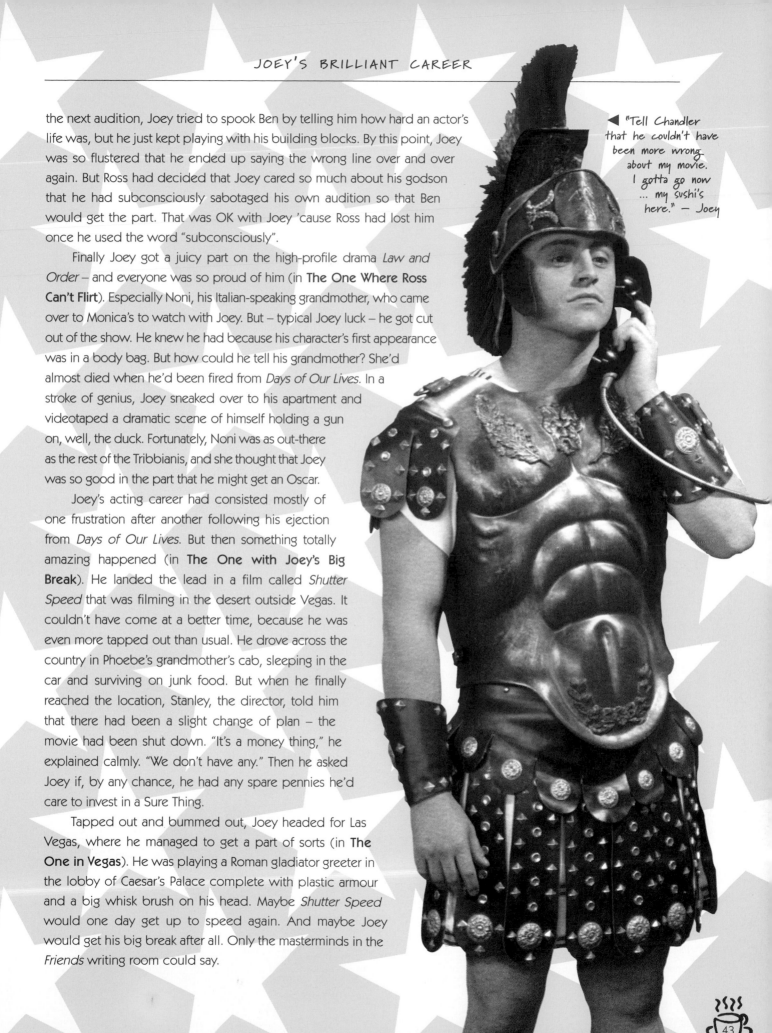

the next audition, Joey tried to spook Ben by telling him how hard an actor's life was, but he just kept playing with his building blocks. By this point, Joey was so flustered that he ended up saying the wrong line over and over again. But Ross had decided that Joey cared so much about his godson that he had subconsciously sabotaged his own audition so that Ben would get the part. That was OK with Joey 'cause Ross had lost him once he used the word "subconsciously".

Finally Joey got a juicy part on the high-profile drama *Law and Order* – and everyone was so proud of him (in **The One Where Ross Can't Flirt**). Especially Noni, his Italian-speaking grandmother, who came over to Monica's to watch with Joey. But – typical Joey luck – he got cut out of the show. He knew he had because his character's first appearance was in a body bag. But how could he tell his grandmother? She'd almost died when he'd been fired from *Days of Our Lives*. In a stroke of genius, Joey sneaked over to his apartment and videotaped a dramatic scene of himself holding a gun on, well, the duck. Fortunately, Noni was as out-there as the rest of the Tribbianis, and she thought that Joey was so good in the part that he might get an Oscar.

Joey's acting career had consisted mostly of one frustration after another following his ejection from *Days of Our Lives*. But then something totally amazing happened (in **The One with Joey's Big Break**). He landed the lead in a film called *Shutter Speed* that was filming in the desert outside Vegas. It couldn't have come at a better time, because he was even more tapped out than usual. He drove across the country in Phoebe's grandmother's cab, sleeping in the car and surviving on junk food. But when he finally reached the location, Stanley, the director, told him that there had been a slight change of plan – the movie had been shut down. "It's a money thing," he explained calmly. "We don't have any." Then he asked Joey if, by any chance, he had any spare pennies he'd care to invest in a Sure Thing.

Tapped out and bummed out, Joey headed for Las Vegas, where he managed to get a part of sorts (in **The One in Vegas**). He was playing a Roman gladiator greeter in the lobby of Caesar's Palace complete with plastic armour and a big whisk brush on his head. Maybe *Shutter Speed* would one day get up to speed again. And maybe Joey would get his big break after all. Only the masterminds in the *Friends* writing room could say.

◄ "Tell Chandler that he couldn't have been more wrong about my movie. I gotta go now ... my sushi's here." — Joey

43

THE SECOND SEASON

Things had become so crazy by the beginning of the second season of *Friends* that Phoebe had to provide a little deep background at the start of the first episode (in **The One with Ross's New Girlfriend**). "Ross has been in love with Rachel since for ever," she explained, "but something always got in the way – like cats or Italian guys. So when Ross was away on a dig, Chandler let slip that Ross was in love with her and Rachel was, like, oh my god."

But when Ross returned from China, he was accompanied by Julie, a Chinese-American palaeontologist. Sussing out the situation immediately, Rachel tried to duck out of the waiting area unnoticed, but instead ended up falling over a chair and cutting her head.

The gang felt terrible for Rachel, while at the same time knowing that they had to be friendly to Julie for

> "Ross has been in love with Rachel since for ever," Phoebe explained, "but something always got in the way – like cats or Italian guys."

Ross's sake. But Rachel had her own prescription for what ailed her: she went right out and dug up bad boy Paolo for a little sexual healing, meanwhile dreaming up ways to sabotage poor, clueless Julie. For example, when Ross confided to Rachel that tonight was the night he was going to have "the sex" with Julie for the first time, Rachel talked her into telling everyone her really long, really boring life story.

What hurt Rachel most was finding out that Monica had betrayed her by going shopping with Julie at Bloomingdale's (in **The One with the Breast Milk**). Monica pleaded with Rachel to cut her a little slack. Julie was her brother's girlfriend. What was she supposed to do?

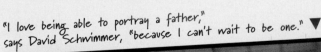

"I love being able to portray a father," says David Schwimmer, "because I can't wait to be one." ▼

▲ Rachel lets Joey talk her into telling Ross that she has "the feelings" for him.

► Ross presents Julie for the gang's approval.

In **The One Where Heckles Dies**, the gang was forced to face the death of someone very close to them – crazy Mr Heckles from downstairs. It seemed like only yesterday that he'd come up to complain about their making too much noise and disturbing his (imaginary) birds – maybe because it was only yesterday. Later, when he'd banged on the ceiling, they'd stomped him into silence. Or they thought they had. Apparently friendless, he had left all his worldly junk to the "noisy girls upstairs". Amid the debris they discovered his wacky quasi-autobiography, "Mr Heckles' Big Book of Grievances", along with his high school annual. When they looked him up, they found that Mr Heckles had not only looked remarkably normal in high school, he had been the "class clown". To his horror, Chandler realized that he and Mr Heckles had a great deal in common. Not only had they both been class cut-ups, it seemed that no woman had been good enough for Mr Heckles, either. That did it. Chandler knew now that he *was* Mr Heckles, and he was going to die just like him – a lonely, embittered, old fruitcake. This thought threw him into such a profound funk that he called (who else?) Janice.

In **The One with Phoebe's Husband**, Phoebe revealed that she had once been married to a gay ice-dancer named Duncan. Not one to be outdone in the secrets department, Chandler grudgingly acknowledged that he had a third nipple; and Joey cheerfully admitted that he had been in a porn movie – which

First it was Nana, then it was Mr Heckles who had passed on to Friends rerun heaven. ▼

▲ If Mr Heckles was going to accuse the girls of stomping, they might as well get a little fun out of it. How could they know it would kill him?

25 September 1995
"Why Is Matthew Perry Still Searching for Ms. Right?" People magazine asked in 1995.
"Ultimately, I'm subscribing to the theory that love will happen when you don't look for it," he answered. "I have finally stopped thinking that there is The One. Boy, I love that idea, but I actually believe that there are 12,000 Ms Rights out there and it's all in the timing."

23 September 1995
"What makes the show special is the six of us," Matthew Perry told TV Guide. "We look like we are having a great time. Because we are."

JFK Jr.: A new career and a hot romance

SEPTEMBER 25, 1995

Nancy Kerrigan weds her agent

People weekly

Chyna & Billy: Happily hitched

FRIENDS' MATTHEW PERRY

He's cute! He's charming! Mothers love him! So why is the wiseacre star of TV's hottest sitcom still searching for Ms. Right?

TV GUIDE **Sneak Peek!**
Special Preview of Your 35 Returning Favorites
Sept. 23–29 99¢

FRIENDS

Season surprises: The big romance, the tiny bundle, and the really bad hairdo

▲ Not only did the three monied Friends go to a Hootie and the Blowfish concert without the others, they also went to the band party afterwards — where Monica got a hickey from an unidentified member of the Blowfish.

Chandler, good friend that he was, managed to dig up for everyone's enjoyment.

The good news in **The One with Five Steaks and an Eggplant** was that a few of the group were starting to earn more money. (The bad news was that the rest of them weren't.) Ross at the museum. Chandler as a programmer. And Monica as a sous-chef at a fancy restaurant. They weren't rich, but they were flush enough for Chandler casually to suggest that they all chip in $62 for a birthday present for Ross. No problem, Joey told him,

▲ "Here's the deal: we lost a car seat on a bus today. It was white plastic with a handle, and it fits on to a stroller. Oh, and there was a baby in it." — Joey

Your friends don't always know everything about you. Even your best friends. Like, for instance, Monica had no idea that Phoebe had been married to Duncan – even though they had been roommates at the time. Phoebe never told Monica because she was sure she'd be judgemental. "Of course I wouldn't approve!" Monica howled. "I mean, you were totally in love with this guy, who was – hello? – gay." It wasn't like it was any big deal, Phoebe said, she was just helping Duncan get his green card. Monica reminded her that she was so depressed when he left that she stayed in her pyjamas for a month.

Friends honcho Kevin S. Bright says that for him, the most exciting guest star ever was Chrissie Hynde. "I had been a Pretenders fan for so long", he recalls, "that I was like a little kid the first day she came to the set. I mean, here is this woman who I'd always thought was the sexiest, greatest singer that I could ever imagine — and she was on my television show."

he'd just sell a kidney. Yeah, and Phoebe and Rachel would be in line right behind him. Ross's birthday dinner at a pricey restaurant made the laggards feel even more self-conscious.

In an effort to smooth things over, Monica brought home the fixings for a great (free) meal for everyone: steaks she'd got from a meat distributor at work and an aubergine (eggplant) for Phoebe, the vegetarian. And that wasn't all: she, Ross and Chandler had chipped in to get them all tickets to a Hootie and the Blowfish concert. Unfortunately, that made the others feel even more like charity cases – although tensions did ease a little when Monica was fired for accepting the steaks. Now she was as badly off as they were.

By **The One with the Baby on the Bus**, Chandler and Joey's attention was back where it usually was – on women. And they didn't let the fact that Ross had entrusted them with the job of babysitting for his son get in the way. They were so focused on the task at hand that they left Ben on a bus – while they followed the trail of two hot-looking babes. Luckily they were able to retrieve Ben at the Transit Authority. At least, they thought it was him.

Meanwhile, in a quest for closure, Rachel left a drunken message for Ross on his answering machine (in **The One Where Ross Finds Out**) – telling him that she was finally over him. Ross

◀ It finally happens ...
the long-awaited kiss.

was completely boggled by this piece of information, since he'd always thought Rachel was oblivious to him. That's why he'd found himself a new girlfriend. But even the slightest possibility of being with Rachel wasn't something he could just ignore.

Chandler had very little sympathy for a man whose problem was having one incredible girlfriend too many, but he did know how Ross could solve the problem. In **The One with the List,** he suggested that Ross tally up Rachel and Julie's pros and cons. Ultimately Ross had no choice but to tell Julie the truth. She cried. He cried. She threw a few things. And then mercifully it was over.

In the meantime, Phoebe was crushed to discover (in **The One with Phoebe's Dad**) that her real father wasn't that handsome-looking guy in the photos they put in the frames in frame stores, but a pharmacist living in upstate New York. She borrowed her grandmother's cab and drove for hours to confront him, but once she was there she couldn't bring herself to ring the bell.

Ross thought things couldn't get any worse until Carol gave him the news that she and her lover, Susan, were getting married (in **The One with the Lesbian Wedding**) Even though all his friends were going to be there, and Monica was going to cater the reception, Ross didn't think he could handle the whole thing. But when Carol's parents refused to attend the wedding, it was so painful that it shattered Carol and Susan's resolve and their spirit. To his own surprise as much as theirs, it was Ross who ended up counselling the two women to get back together.

Ross had a touching reunion with Marcel the monkey in **The One After the Superbowl.** Since leaving Ross, Marcel had become a thespian with several impressive films to his credit. Ross and the gang stopped by to see Marcel while he was filming his latest – an action thriller co-starring Jean-Claude Van Damme.

In a nifty piece of casting, Marta Kauffman and David Crane got Candace Gingrich, the lesbian sister of Newt Gingrich, the Republican Speaker of the House at that time, to play the minister at Carol and Susan's wedding.

▼ "Oh my god, now I've seen everything!" Carol and Susan's wedding was interrupted by an outburst from a little old (dead) lady named Rose Adelman — whose spirit had taken possession of Phoebe.

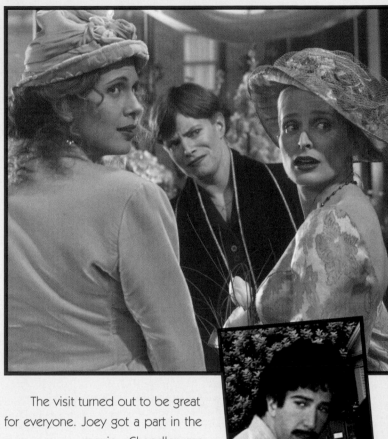

▲ Ross almost had a chance with Rachel when her prom date turned up late in The One with the Prom Video.

The visit turned out to be great for everyone. Joey got a part in the movie. Chandler ran into a luscious-looking girl (guest star Julia Roberts) he hadn't seen since grade school. Ross got Marcel to himself for a whole day. And Rachel got a date with the mighty Jean-Claude. Never mind that she was supposed to be interceding on Monica's behalf with Muscle Boy.

In **The One with the Prom Video,** Phoebe found an old home video shot on the night of Rachel and Monica's senior high school prom – a fun occasion, except that Rachel seemed to have been stood up by

◄ Former model and child actress Brooke Shields got a chance to show off her comedic talents to television audiences for the first time on Friends. Her role as Erica the stalker helped Brooke to land her own Warner Bros. series, Suddenly Susan. Here she hangs with another model-turned-actress on the set of The One with Two Parts.

COSTUME DESIGN

Friends costume designer Debra McGuire's fashion stories for the six Friends were glamorous while still reflecting the casual approach favoured by their real-life contemporaries. Their clothes – jeans and T-shirts, ankle-length skirts, etc. – not only helped to define their characters, but helped to generate a number of hip new trends.

The three female Friends are Debra McGuire's very own life-sized Barbie Dolls and there's nothing she likes better than having a script call for one of them to be seen in something extravagant for a special occasion. The figure-hugging gown on the left was dreamed up for Monica to wear to a New Year's Eve party during the first season and the filmy creation on the right was created for Phoebe's appearance in her first (and final) music video for "Smelly Cat."

her date. He turned up eventually, but not before Ross had changed into his dad's tuxedo so that he could save the day. Everyone was touched, but none more so than Rachel – who had been totally unaware of Ross's good-hearted gesture at the time. She walked slowly over to Ross, took his face in her hands and kissed him deeply on the lips.

After several awkward attempts to get physical in **The One Where Ross and Rachel ... You Know**, Ross and Rachel finally managed to consummate – and deeply enjoy – their first sexual encounter. (Even if it was in a diorama at the Museum of Natural History.) The night was so romantic that they almost didn't mind waking up to find themselves being ogled by a group of giggling elementary school kids.

▲ Rachel and Monica play paper-rock-scissors for the last of the condoms – while Ross and Richard wait not-at-all patiently.

◄ When Joey's soap picked up his option, he celebrated by buying matching Lazy-Boy recliner chairs for himself and Chandler.

"Coming up with funny lines for Jean-Claude Van Damme was quite a challenge. We had these funny lines, but they weren't funny on him. So we had to come up with lines that were Van Damme-proof. So I would say them in a really horrible French accent, putting the emphasis on the wrong word, and if people still laughed, then we pitched them to Van Damme. And that's how we came up with his 'I can crack a walnut with my butt'" - *Friends* writer

To their surprise, the producers of *Friends* had to haggle long and hard with NBC's Standards and Practices Department in order to keep the scene in The One Where Dr Ramoray Dies where Monica and Rachel fought over the last condom. "We thought we were giving such a great message," says writer Greg Malins. "When you think of *Friends*, you think of responsible sex."

Joey now had a continuing part as the handsome neurosurgeon Dr Drake Ramoray in *Days of Our Lives*. His soapy payday was so lush that he decided the time had come to move himself into a soap-opera-star-worthy pad. It wasn't like Chandler wasn't still his best bud, but he had been plenty crabby lately, blowing up over stupid things – like Joey's licking the spoons instead of washing them. Joey's departure was deeply hurtful to Chandler. But once Joey had made the move, he was surprised to find himself getting lonely. He thought he'd like being alone with his thoughts, but realized he didn't really have any. Chandler was lonely, too – so much so that he started having conversations with his fuzzy puppy house slippers. So he pulled himself together (in **The One Where Eddie Moves In**) and recruited a new roommate – a guy named Eddie he had met in the ethnic foods section of a supermarket.

Joey was incensed when he saw Eddie cooking breakfast in the kitchen of his old apartment and acting as if he had always lived there. But Eddie turned out to be anything but Chandler's dream roommate. For one thing, he didn't like foose-ball or *Baywatch*. And, instead of vegging in front of the tube like a normal guy, he retreated to his bedroom to do strange things – like read a book. That left Joey and Chandler sitting forlornly in front of their big screen TVs at opposite ends of town, watching *Baywatch*…alone, together.

The longer Eddie was around, the more obvious it became to Chandler that he was a secret psycho. Not a particularly brave soul under the best of circumstances, Chandler started spending the night on Monica and Rachel's couch across the hall. By this point, Chandler was missing Joey more than

▲ Believe it or not, new roommate Eddie seemed normal in the beginning.

"It was crazy what happened with the studio audience when Tom Selleck hit the stage," remembers director Michael Lembeck, shown here directing Selleck and Courteney Cox in The One Where Ross and Rachel ... You Know. "It was like The Beatles with the screaming and the applause. We had to reshoot his entrance after the audience had gone home on all the shows he did with us."

◀ Ross comforts Rachel as they watch the heart-wrenching ending of Old Yeller.

▼ The longer Eddie was around, the more obvious it became to Chandler that he was a secret psycho.

ever. As luck would have it, Joey had already managed to get himself fired from *Days of Our Lives*. But he was so humiliated by getting bounced that he hadn't told anyone. The good news was that he could now move back in with Chandler. In fact, he had to – seeing as he'd got himself deeply in debt while playing rich TV star. The guys would have to get Eddie out first, though. But that was easy enough. In **The One Where Eddie Won't Go**, Chandler came up with the nifty idea of simply changing the locks and "reminding" Eddie that he had already moved out. Fortunately for them Eddie remembered.

By **The One Where Old Yeller Dies**, Ross was feeling left out of baby Ben's life. So he asked Carol and Susan for more time with his son. He had barely got the

23 December 1995 TV Guide salutes the fabulous Friends follicles.

February 1996 US magazine creates a special fold-out cover for the "Supervixens of Friends ... and the Men Who Love Them".

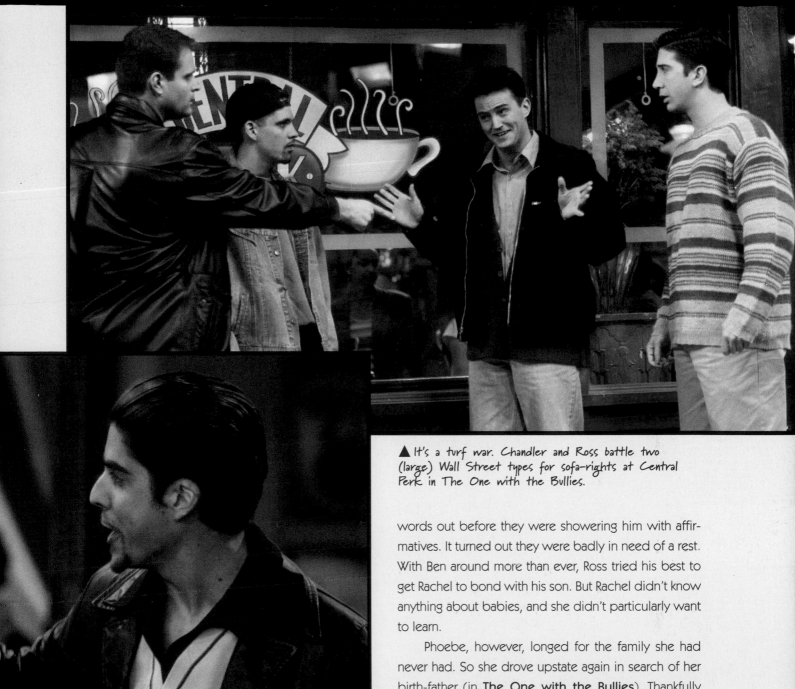

▲ It's a turf war. Chandler and Ross battle two (large) Wall Street types for sofa-rights at Central Perk in **The One with the Bullies.**

words out before they were showering him with affirmatives. It turned out they were badly in need of a rest. With Ben around more than ever, Ross tried his best to get Rachel to bond with his son. But Rachel didn't know anything about babies, and she didn't particularly want to learn.

Phoebe, however, longed for the family she had never had. So she drove upstate again in search of her birth-father (in **The One with the Bullies**). Thankfully she had Joey and Rachel with her this time to provide moral support. After some words of encouragement from them when they arrived, she took a deep breath and headed for her father's house. But just as she was about to knock on the door, she was attacked by the family's demented little dog. Seeing this as a bad sign,

The Ultimate Good-Deed Guide • Sex and Weather
Secret B&B's • Computer Shopping • Sixers Road Trip
Philadelphia
'Friends' from Home
Meet the Philadelphia duo behind TV's hottest show
By Amy Donohue

February 1996
Hometown Kids Make Good (TV). Although they had long since moved on to L.A. by the time *Philadelphia* magazine premiered this story, everybody back home in Philly was more-than-happy to claim Marta Kauffman and David Crane, the hot writing duo who'd created *Friends,* as their very own.

"The One with Two Parties was a very difficult episode to pin down," remembers *Friends* co-creator David Crane, "because, really, the show isn't about broad comedy. But we realized that we had to embrace the sheer farce of all the people sneaking around and yet somehow still combine it with the heart of the story – which played out between Rachel and Chandler in the hall."

▶ Rachel's mother (guest star Marlo Thomas) had split up with her husband and was ready to start her new life in The One with Two Parties.

Phoebe bailed again, but, in her haste, she ended up running over the Buffays' family pet. Fortunately the dog pulled through, and Phoebe's only problem was explaining what had happened when she delivered him back to the Buffay house. After handing over the dog to the frowsy woman (guest star Laraine Newman) who'd answered the door, she timidly asked for Frank. "Fra-a-ank!" the woman yelled and a dorky teenage boy ambled out. Phoebe said she guessed she meant Frank Sr. "He went out for groceries," the woman said, "four years ago." OK, so she'd lost her father's trail again, but wow, she had a half-brother! And there was something kind of wonderful about that.

Rachel had to deal with family trauma, too (in **The One with Two Parties**) after getting the sad news that her parents were getting divorced. She knew she was supposed to be too adult to let this sort of thing get to her, but her parents' break-up made her feel like a little lost kid. The gang tried to cheer her up with a surprise party, but the real surprise was that both her parents decided to come, too. If Rachel wanted to avoid a huge blow-up that would embarrass her in front of all her friends, she had to keep them from finding out that the other one was there. That meant improvising two parties – one at Monica's for Mrs Green – and another at Joey and Chandler's for Dr Green. This plan was so complicated that Ross begged her to put the two parties (and the two parents) together. Monica's soirée was like a remedial workshop for the socially stiff – whereas the boys' do was a raucous funfest with pizza and dancing and pick-up volleyball. Oh yeah, and Rachel's dad. Hearing the merry-making across the hall made Monica's guests desperate to make a break for the fun party, so Phoebe took pity on them and sneaked out as many as she could. Finally Rachel's parents decided to leave – at the same time, of course. But the guys managed to keep them apart with an intricately staged troop movement. As Dr Green moved out into the hall, the group

Demi's Naked Truth • 'Celestine' Profiteering
Entertainment WEEKLY
The Friends Nerd Shoots For Movie Stardom
Can David Schwimmer Go Hollywood?

26 April 1996 The answer is yes. David Schwimmer talks to Entertainment Weekly about his extra-Friends-curricular activities.

Ryan (guest star Charlie Sheen) and Phoebe can't stop scratching when they both come down with chicken pox.

surrounded him and moved him down the stairs. Meanwhile, Joey diverted Mrs Green by pinning her to the wall and giving her a big wet kiss.

As much would be blasted apart in this final episode (**The One with Barry and Mindy's Wedding**) as would be resolved. Unhappily for Monica, this would be the episode that bid farewell to Richard. But she had realized that, if she stayed with Richard, she would have to sacrifice her desire to have children. And somewhere on some unidentified part of Long Island, Rachel was preparing to be a part of the wedding party for Barry and Mindy's nuptials. Naturally she was a little uptight because the last wedding she'd

"Back during *Friends'* first season, Courteney Cox was asked why her character hadn't got involved with either Joey or Chandler and she answered, "Monica's too smart to sleep with Joey, and Chandler doesn't know how to have a relationship."

been to with Barry had been her own. And if that weren't bad enough, she had to wear a frothy pink dress with big puffed sleeves that made her look like Princess Bubble Yum. But she had to put in an appearance. And anyway, what was the worst that could happen? Well, she could have walked down the aisle with the back of her skirt tucked into her panties and her backside completely exposed. And then she could have stood up on the bandstand and started singing "Copacabana" for no apparent reason. Barry's family had told the guests that Rachel had gone insane (from syphilis) after running out on their wedding. So that explained her behaviour ...

▲ Barry told Rachel that his family had told everyone she had gone insane (from syphilis) after she ran out on their wedding.

July 1996
And US obviously can't get enough of Courteney Cox either. It's easy to see why she's one of the magazine's favourite cover girls.

COURTENEY COX PROFILE

Courteney Cox has two lovers – and she ain't ashamed. Yes, the lovely Courteney has found her soul mates both on and off screen with her marriage to *Scream* co-star David Arquette, and her high-voltage romance with Chandler Bing. "It's my favourite year," she says of *Friends*' fifth season. "I've had so much to play. I've loved my storyline. I'm just glad that the audience has accepted it and loves it so much, because it's just so much fun for me."

Courteney Cox can now step comfortably into the *Friends*' spotlight after doing her best to deflect it during the show's first year. She was the cast member with the name, the track record, not to mention the one who'd boogied with the Boss, so it was taken for granted that she was the star of the show's cast of then-unknowns. She set out to kill off that potentially disruptive vibe with a pre-emptive strike. "She was actually the first person to speak up about us being a team," Matthew Perry says. "It was our second day at work, and we went outside on a break together and she said, 'This is an ensemble show. I think we should really all try to help each other out.' Everybody just jumped on that." She might have been sensitive about this sort of thing because she herself had been odd man out in a show on which the star pecking order was firmly entrenched, having made her entrance into *Family Ties* five years into its awesome seven-year run.

While the *Friends* producers were correct in creating an ensemble set-up for their cast, they were a trifle off the mark with regard to at least one thing: they wanted Courteney Cox to play Rachel. "They said, 'We see you more as Rachel,'" She remembers, "but I would have played Rachel as much more neurotic, and I wouldn't have been as good as Jennifer."

Courteney Cox was born in 1964 in the country-club suburbs of Birmingham, Alabama, the youngest of four children (two sisters, Virginia and Dottie, and one brother, Richard). Her parents divorced when she was ten years old. Both parents remarried two years later and

> **"I'm not a quirky person, although I'd like to be. I think it looks fun to be quirky, but I just don't have it in me. I'm working towards being a kook."**
> *Courteney Cox*

> **"Monica is not only neurotic and nutty and whatever,"** says Courteney Cox, **"but she's also sexual and mature. So she can kind of teach Chandler the ropes as opposed to being the insecure female."**

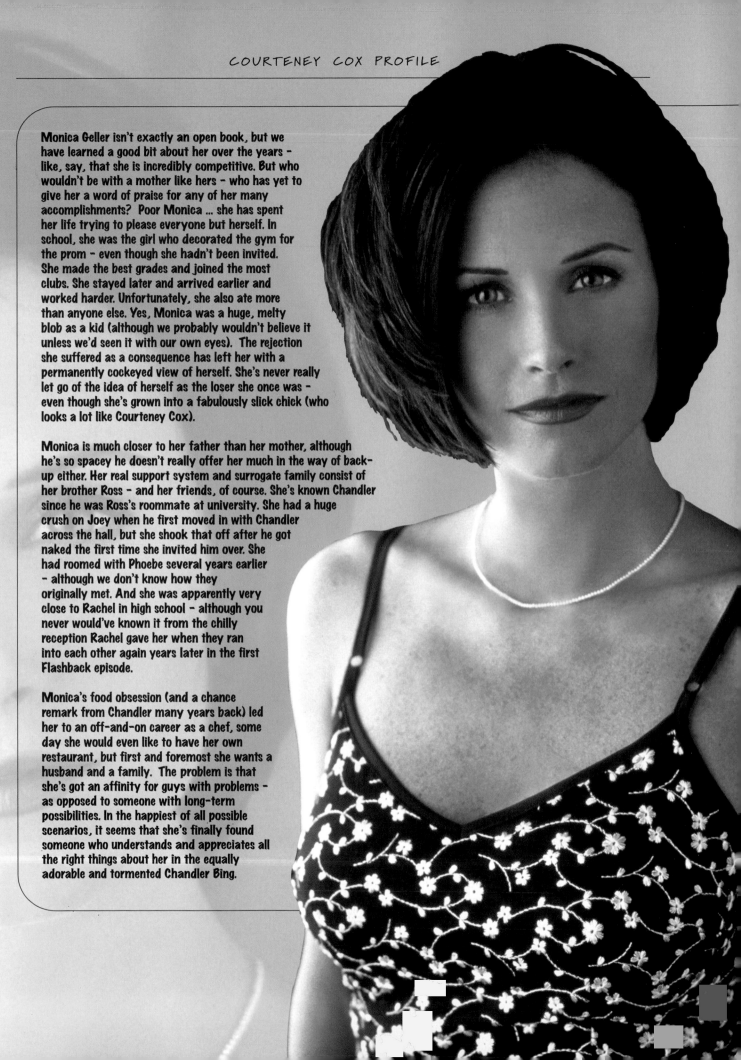

Monica Geller isn't exactly an open book, but we have learned a good bit about her over the years – like, say, that she is incredibly competitive. But who wouldn't be with a mother like hers – who has yet to give her a word of praise for any of her many accomplishments? Poor Monica ... she has spent her life trying to please everyone but herself. In school, she was the girl who decorated the gym for the prom – even though she hadn't been invited. She made the best grades and joined the most clubs. She stayed later and arrived earlier and worked harder. Unfortunately, she also ate more than anyone else. Yes, Monica was a huge, melty blob as a kid (although we probably wouldn't believe it unless we'd seen it with our own eyes). The rejection she suffered as a consequence has left her with a permanently cockeyed view of herself. She's never really let go of the idea of herself as the loser she once was – even though she's grown into a fabulously slick chick (who looks a lot like Courteney Cox).

Monica is much closer to her father than her mother, although he's so spacey he doesn't really offer her much in the way of back-up either. Her real support system and surrogate family consist of her brother Ross – and her friends, of course. She's known Chandler since he was Ross's roommate at university. She had a huge crush on Joey when he first moved in with Chandler across the hall, but she shook that off after he got naked the first time she invited him over. She had roomed with Phoebe several years earlier – although we don't know how they originally met. And she was apparently very close to Rachel in high school – although you never would've known it from the chilly reception Rachel gave her when they ran into each other again years later in the first Flashback episode.

Monica's food obsession (and a chance remark from Chandler many years back) led her to an off-and-on career as a chef, some day she would even like to have her own restaurant, but first and foremost she wants a husband and a family. The problem is that she's got an affinity for guys with problems – as opposed to someone with long-term possibilities. In the happiest of all possible scenarios, it seems that she's finally found someone who understands and appreciates all the right things about her in the equally adorable and tormented Chandler Bing.

The original script for **The One with Ross's Wedding** in the fourth season called for Monica to plant the seeds of discontent in Emily in this scene at the bridal shop. The scene was cut, but fortunately fans got to see Monica in her slinky red bridesmaid gown at the wedding.

nine stepchildren were added to the mix. "I think because my parents did get divorced, I felt there were a lot of things I had to accomplish," she has said. "I think I grew up fast, not necessarily emotionally, but I had to take care of myself." Although there were mild episodes of rebelliousness, she stuck to the straight and narrow – graduating from high school and then enrolling in college, where she intended to study to become an architect. But in the summer before her freshman year she took the advice of her stepfather's brother, Miles Copeland Sr, a former CIA operative who – guided perhaps by her beauty, perhaps by her drive – strongly advised her to go to New York before grounding herself in a traditional southern life. To her great advantage, Copeland Sr's sons would provide support and serious entrées for the callow Alabama girl. Miles Jr, President of IRS records; Ian, the head of FBI, New York's trendiest rock'n'roll booking agency; and Stewart, the drummer and co-founder of the Police, had become three of the most powerful players in the music business.

With the help of the Copeland clan, Courteney landed a contract with the prestigious Ford modelling agency and went on to become one of those fresh-faced girls whose sunny countenances appear on teen magazines like *Tiger Beat* and *Young Miss* as well as the covers of romance novels aimed at young women.

After a summer in New York she went to Washington, DC to attend her freshman year in college. She then returned to New York, where she filmed commercials for Noxema, Maybelline and most notably Tampax, wherein she made TV history by uttering the then-forbidden word "period", referring to her menstrual cycle as opposed to that little dot at the end of a sentence. She also landed a two-day walk-on part as a debutante named

When she's working, Monica Geller is seen in her chef's smock and toque. For her at-home wear, costume designer Debra McGuire tends to dress her size 2 frame in casual body-hugging jeans, capri pants and leotard-style tops in a colour palette of black, grey, navy and burgundy, plum and red. Like Rachel, she has a cleavage and is not above showing her belly once in a while.

Bunny on the long-running New York soap opera, *As the World Turns*. All this while she was preparing herself for bigger things ... taking speech lessons to lose her southern accent and acting lessons so as to negotiate the well-travelled path from model to actress. And then came the legendary Big Break for which she remains famous today. In 1984, she went to a casting "cattle call" for a brief cameo in a Bruce Springsteen video in which the script called for the Boss to pull a fan up on to the stage for a flirtatious pas-de-deux. "There were lots of dancers there ... these great long-legged women, and I'm wearing jeans and sneakers, and I went, 'Whoa, I'm in the wrong place.'" But the video's director Brian de Palma wanted the little interlude to look like a piece of video verite´ and that meant choosing a girl who looked like the

> **"If you actually lived with Monica, you'd have to kill her."**
> *Courteney Cox*

real thing. All told, she was in the video only 26 seconds, but her bashful Every Girl created an indelible image that endures to this day. She says now that the part didn't change her fortunes all that radically, but it did open a lot of doors. And no doubt it earned her extra Cool Points with the very hip producers of *Friends*. "After [the video] I lived in New York, and people would want me to tell them what Bruce was really like. Are you Bruce's sister? Are you his girlfriend? Who are you?"

In 1985 she signed on to *Misfits of Science* – her first TV series. But neither the show, nor her first two feature-film outings – *Down Twisted* and *Masters of the*

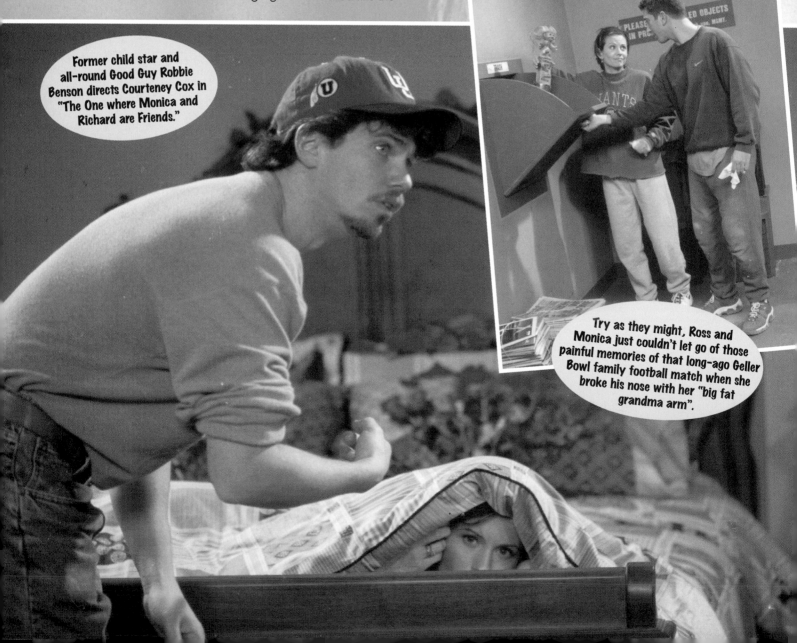

Former child star and all-round Good Guy Robbie Benson directs Courteney Cox in "The One where Monica and Richard are Friends."

Try as they might, Ross and Monica just couldn't let go of those painful memories of that long-ago Geller Bowl family football match when she broke his nose with her "big fat grandma arm".

Universe – did her any justice. It was her role as Lauren, Michael J. Fox's girlfriend, in *Family Ties* that brought her to America's attention once again. Several film appearances (*Cocoon: the Return* and *Mr Destiny*) led to the low-budget quickie *Ace Ventura: Pet Detective* – one of the all-time comedy blockbusters. Yet, despite her presence in several high-profile comedies, the world really had no idea that the lovely Courteney could be funny. It was not until her inspired turn as Monica Geller that it became apparent that this babe could not only act, she could also get laughs.

"Let's face it," she once said in defence of Monica's insecurities, "we've all got problems. We don't choose the right people, we've all got hang-ups. It's hard in life anyway to find the right person."

Well, that's what she said a couple of years ago – before she found exactly the right person in David Arquette. Their wedding ceremony was a traditional one that took place at the historic Grace Cathedral atop ritzy Nob Hill in San Francisco, with hundreds of friends and family there to wish them well. The bride and groom then returned to the set of *Scream 3* to finish shooting. Which was fine with all of us – so long as she made it back in good time for the sixth season of *Friends*.

Close enough: Chandler had pinned his marriage proposal to Monica to her rolling a "Hard Eight". When one die bounced off the crap table and landed on the floor beneath, he made the call in the marriage's favour.

Are these real? Matthew Perry checks out Courteney Cox's awesome physique on the set of The One with All the Jealousy.

THE THIRD SEASON

The third season of *Friends* began with Ross discovering to his horror that Rachel had told Monica and Phoebe about his Princess Leia fantasy. Women tell each other things like that all the time, she told him. Maybe the guys were missing out on something by not communicating on an intimate level. So they decided to try their luck at sharing. Ross started the bidding with his fantasy of getting up close and personal with Galactic royalty, then Chandler upped the ante by saying how when he was having sex, a picture of his mom sometimes popped into his mind. This was not only too intimate for Ross, it was downright disgusting. Later that night when Rachel got herself all done up in authentic Princess Leia drag, all Ross could see was Judy Geller (his mother). He couldn't explain his sudden loss of enthusiasm to Rachel – other than to say he hated Chandler.

Comparatively speaking, the problems in the next few episodes were pretty mild. If only things could have stayed that simple.

Monica, panicky that she would never find the right man to father her children now that Richard was out of

◄ *Jack Geller has a heart-to-heart with his "Little Harmonica."*

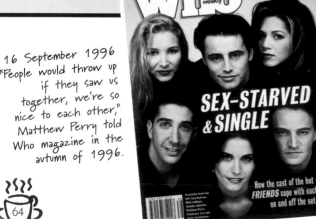

16 September 1996 "People would throw up if they saw us together, we're so nice to each other," Matthew Perry told Who magazine in the autumn of 1996.

Courtesy of WHO WEEKLY

"Hey, you were great, too." The cast applauds the audience after completing The One Where No One's Ready.

She loves him, she loves him not. It was only a few minutes ago in *The One Where No One's Ready* that Rachel was refusing to get dressed for Ross's big museum event because she wasn't in "a museum-benefitty mood".

THE ULTIMATE FRIENDS COMPANION

◀ "Either you're seeing someone behind my back, or you're pretending you're seeing someone behind my back — which is so pathetic I could just start crying right here in the cereal aisle." — Janice

"You mean I can have sex with you, but I can't touch you?" an incredulous Frank Jr asks his masseuse, Jasmine. ▼

her life, came *that close* to being inseminated with anonymous donor sperm in **The One with the Jam**. But on the day she was leaving for the sperm bank, Joey happened to ask her what the guy she'd picked was like. "Dark hair, green eyes," she answered. Funny, Joey said, he'd always imagined her with a blond guy — with a swimmer's body and a name like Hoyt. And by the time he had finished, she had realized just what she would be missing without a dad.

While Monica was berating herself for being alone, Chandler was chafing from too much togetherness in **The One with the Metaphorical Tunnel**. Janice, he complained, was starting to act as if they were an old married couple. Instead of running away, as was his usual custom, he decided (thanks to Rachel and Monica's tutelage) he was going to try commitment. He was so determined to turn over a new leaf that he even made a place for Janice to keep her things in his apartment. Then it was Janice's turn to get cold feet. After all, she hadn't even got a divorce from her husband yet.

Matthew Perry finds a novel place to stash his telephone on the set of The One with All the Jealousy.

Rachel tells her friends that what she needs is meaningless sex with the next guy she sees.

While the others struggled with affairs of the heart, Phoebe was slowly but surely beginning to reassemble the family she never had (in **The One with Frank Jr**). The first piece of the Buffay family puzzle to fall into place was Frank Jr – whom she had found while trying to smoke out her father. They'd got along really well at that first meeting, communicating in their own bizarre Buffay language. Hoping to do a little more bonding with Frank Jr, she invited him down to New York for the weekend. But mostly all they did was to sit together in silence. The next day, Phoebe decided to take Frank Jr along to her job – which he was impressed to learn was at a massage parlour. "We don't call it that," Phoebe interjected, but he was already off on his own fantasy trip. When Phoebe told Frank Jr she was going to treat him to a massage, he told her she was the "best sister ever". He quickly got in trouble for trying to touch his masseuse, Jasmine. Phoebe was incensed when she realized what her brother thought she did for a living. The time had come for him to go home. But Frank Jr was having a perfect time he told her, in that he could really talk to her … because she was his sister.

The One with the Flashback was set three years earlier in the lives of the Friends, but in some ways things weren't all that different.

If you had a freebie with any five people in the world, who would you choose? Ross chose Isabella Rossellini. Or he would have — if she only hung out in America more. Imagine his surprise when the genuine article ambled into The One with Frank Jr. The producers — here with Rossellini during a rehearsal break — were pretty pleased about it too. ▼

"For me," says *Friends* co-creator David Crane, "the hardest part of The One with the Flashback was trying to get Phoebe to the point where she would believably kiss Ross. They're so much like brother and sister that it seemed incestuous.

THE FANS

The fans not only write in, but they give their views on-line too. Why not visit the official *Friends* website at http://friends.warnerbros.com or one of the many *Friends* chatrooms?

> Friends Online Chatroom

> Name:Kieren
> From: California
> Comments: I is likened this cause it has pictures of sexy Ross

> Name: Ali
> From:Scotland
> Comments: Friends is fab! Phoebe is so funny - I love her songs! Joey and Chandler just crack me up - they could have a show all to themselves. Can't wait for the next series. Oh, Monica and Rachel are okay too, but Ross is the resident annoying character.

> Name: Jo
> From: Planet Nyongong
> Comments: Friends is pretty cool. I also watch Southpark. At the moment I am floating above Earth in my flying saucer linked onto your internet which isn't as sophisticated as the internet on my planet. I love watching The Simpsons too. I have a lovely boyfriend.

> Name: Kirsten
> From: Scotland
> Comments: Get Ross and Rachel back together!

> Name: Katy
> From: England
> Comments; Friends rule the world!!! Esp Chandler

---

c/o "FRIENDS"
BROS. STUDIO
TV PLAZA
136, RM. 226
, CA 91505

Dear Friends cast,

I am a fan of your show + I really like watching the Friends show. So does my friends. We all think you guys make a great job that's why you all have of fans.

I know also that you get plenty of mail but I was wondering if I could please get an autograph from the Friends cast. It would be great!

Well, I hope to hear from soon. I will deeply appreciate generosity in sending me an autograph.

Thanks a lot!

Sincerely,
Jvdtha

P.S.: Since Matthew Perry's b is coming soon I'd like to wish him a HAPPY B-DAY! He's a great actor.

July 30, 1999

c/o "Friends"
Warner Bros. Studio
300 South TV Plaza
Building 136, Room 226
Burbank, CA 91505

To the cast of "Friends"

I just want to say just how much I love your show! Every night I sit down and laugh my sides out. I love the show so much that I record every episode that I watch. Then on the weekends, I can watch them over and over.

You all are such good actors and actresses and you all do such a wonderful job. "Friends" is definitely my all time favorite show. I would never miss an episode.

So keep up the good work, and have a great summer, and I'll be watching you every night at six and ten.

See ya all on TV!

Becki

P.S. You guys have a billboard in Pueblo, Colorado, and you're all on it! Congratulations!

YOUR NUMBER ONE

Dear Cast of "Friends"
First off my family and I are huge fans. We watch faithfully EVERY Thursday at 8:00pm Second off would like to congradulate "Mon (Courtney Cox) on her engageme David Arquette (The AT&T guy). And if you would please, PLEASE send an autographed photo signed by all of you. PLEASE!

Your biggest fans,
The Jewell's
Karen, Raymond,
Abbie, Allie, and
Annie.

P.S. We all think that "R get with "Rachel"

Friends
c/o Warner Bros.
4000 Warner Blvd.
Burbank, California

To: Friends
300 South Television Plaza
Building 136
Suite 226
Burbank, CA 91505

Even the Master of the Universe is a fan of *Friends.*

LUCASFILM Ltd

October 4, 1996

Mr. Kevin Bright
Ms. Marta Kauffman
Mr. David Crane
Executive Producers
Bright, Kauffman and Crane

Dear Kevin, Marta, and David:

I must tell you how much my family and I enjoyed watching the season premiere of "Friends." The Princess Leia fantasy was great! Congratulations on a terrific series and a brilliant season premiere.

Sincerely,

George Lucas

GWL/am

▲ Thank goodness ... Ugly Naked Guy was still alive (but he wasn't happy).

◄ Monica and Rachel had a great time babysitting Ben — until Monica bashed his little head while playing Airplane.

Monica was afraid that her quirks made her unlovable. And Chandler's new roommate Joey took Monica's invitation to make himself comfortable to mean that he should get naked. Oh yeah, and then there was Ross, just broken up with Carol – trying (in the worst way) to have sex with his friend Phoebe on a pool table.

Moving back out of the time warp (for **The One with the Race Car Bed**), Ross allowed Rachel to talk him into going to dinner with her and her father, although he wasn't thrilled. "He hates me," he complained. "He calls me 'Wet Head'." At dinner, Dr Green got things off to a friendly start by asking Ross how things were going at the library. Ross said he supposed they were

September 1996 "The money that people have made out of these tabloid papers and TV shows is unbelievable," Jennifer Aniston told FHM magazine in 1996. "It's the disgusting side of Hollywood. They're always making up fights between the Friends co-stars. There was one in Star magazine that said I was 'The Queen of Mean'. I was, like, 'Whaaaat?!'"

In the October 1996 issue of Seventeen, you could find out what made Matt LeBlanc tick and why guys kiss and run.

▶ During a highly competitive game of touch football, Ross told Rachel to "go long" so many times that she finally went long for a pretzel from a sidewalk vendor.

▲ Watch out, Phoebe — ex-partner Jingle Bitch will sell you out.

fine, but he worked at a museum. It was downhill from there – culminating in an ugly tiff over how much Dr Green should leave for the tip.

Whatever Rachel's shortcomings, bopping baby Ben on the head was not one of them – although she got the blame for doing precisely that in **The One with the Giant Poking Device**. After the much-begged-for babysitting job, Rachel found her hands full of Baby Ben, who was missing daddy. Aunt Monica stepped in to save the day, with a fun game of Airplane, only to bang Ben's head so hard that a noticeable bump appeared on his little head.

Unlike Rachel, Phoebe was more than willing to take the blame for even the most oddball

Men's Fitness, November 199. © Men's Fitness 1996.

He's fit, all right. Matt LeBlanc reveals how he does it in Men's Fitness.

The kid's done pretty well for himself. David Crane's father, Gene, makes an appearance in The One Where Rachel Quits.

occurrences. She even decided that she had killed the Ugly Naked Guy (UNG) whom the gang spied on through their window, because she had gone to the dentist — and with good reason, since every time she'd gone to the dentist in the past, someone had died. (That's why she took such good care of her teeth.) Sure enough, on the day of Phoebe's appointment, Joey noticed that Ugly Naked Guy hadn't moved since early that morning. Phoebe was racked with remorse until Joey figured out a way to prove to her that UNG was OK. He had the bright idea of making an extra-long pole from all of their old chopsticks, which they could use to stick through his window and poke him to see if they could get a response. To her relief, the lifeless body jerked to attention when the giant pole made contact. Hallelujah … Ugly Naked Guy was alive!

The gang's togetherness went kaflooey in **The One with the Football**. Ancient rivalries were re-ignited when the gang gathered together to play what should have been a friendly game of touch football on Thanksgiving Day. Who could have known that Ross and Monica had a football feud that stretched all the way back to their childhood?

Joey's snow-stencilled plea of "PLEH" (help spelled backwards) went unheeded by the freeway police helicopters. ▼

In The One Where Rachel Quits, Ross accidentally broke the leg of an eight-year-old Brown Bird named Sarah — who'd been going door-to-door selling cookies to win a trip to Space Camp so she could sit in a real space shuttle. Determined to win her the trip, Ross took over her cookie route and actually managed to sell 517 boxes of Brown Bird cookies — but was outdone by another Brown Bird who sold 875 boxes.

The debate over whether or not Ross was justified in sleeping with Chloe was argued not just on the show, but in the writers' room – where, for the most part, allegiances corresponded with gender. "We get a lot of stories from this kind of argument," says *Friends* co-creator David Crane. "When you've got a show with six characters who are always talking-talking-talking, you've constantly got to come up with things for them to take sides on."

The game ended up being between the guys and the girls – which, you'd think, would have given the guys quite an advantage. And it did, until Rachel caught a pass in the end zone. But then Chandler pointed out that she had been out of bounds – which meant that the ball was still in play. Both Monica and Ross dived for the fake-pigskin-covered projectile. Later that night, while the rest of the group sat down to the delicious turkey Monica had cooked for them, the Geller siblings were still sprawled on top of the ball as it slowly started to snow.

Ross was back in the soup again in **The One Where Rachel Quits** after he accidentally broke the leg of an eight-year-old Brown Bird named Sarah while demonstrating his backswing to Chandler. Now this Sarah wasn't just any little girl. Oh no. She was a poignant little waif who helped to support her ne'er-do-well father when she wasn't in school studying to become an astronaut one day. And there was more: before Ross clobbered her, she'd been selling cookies door to door to win a trip to Space Camp. (*And* it was Christmas!)

Happily the holiday wasn't doom and gloom for everyone. Phoebe became the foster mother for several dried-up Christmas trees that had been heading for the wood-chipper. And Rachel got a job at a place called Fortunata Fashions – after impetuously quitting her waitressing job at Central Perk.

It turned out that Rachel's duties at Fortunata Fashions consisted mostly of making coffee for the boss and separating hangers. But in **The One Where Chandler Can't Remember**, a cute guy named Mark, who happened to overhear her complaining about the job to Monica, helped her get an interview at Bloomingdale's. Ross had a feeling that Mark's motives weren't all that philanthropic. He met Rachel after the interview – so he was there to hear Mark excitedly give her the good news that she had got the job. She was so excited that she hugged him. Mark, that is.

Ross was sure he had been proved right (in **The One with All the Jealousy**) when he overheard what he

◄ "I can't believe this. This is the most horrible thing that's ever happened ever. I knew something had to be wrong. My fingernails did not grow at all yesterday." – Phoebe on Ross and Rachel's break-up.

thought was Mark and Rachel sweet-talking in her office, but it turned out that Mark was cuddling his own girlfriend while Rachel looked on approvingly. Ross, the jealous fool, burst into the office yelling, "All right, that's it. Get off of her!!"

▲
Chandler wondered if his Easter Chick, Little Yasmine could swim as well as his new duck.

In **The One with Phoebe's Ex-Partner**, it was Phoebe's turn to be jealous – of Leslie, a girl singer who had recently started performing at Central Perk. Leslie had once been Phoebe's singing partner – before abandoning her to work for a jingle house. And Phoebe still bore her a big grudge for selling out. But after the two of them sang a duet of the Phoebe classic, "Sticky Shoes Always Make Me Smile", Phoebe softened towards her. Then she really let her guard down and sang "Smelly Cat", her masterpiece. True to form, Leslie stole "Smelly Cat" and took it to her old agency, taking credit for it as her own.

Ross proves to Rachel that his "Frankie Say Relax" T-shirt still fits.
▼

Rachel tried her best to be tolerant of Ross's insecurity over her new job, until he finally pushed her to the limit on a night when she had to work late. In Ross's defence, it was their anniversary, and Rachel had had to break the special date they'd had for weeks. So he was sure she would think it was romantic when he surprised her at the office with a candlelit dinner. And maybe she would have if he hadn't set fire to the papers on her desk.

When Ross didn't apologize for the catastrophe, Rachel told him that it was time for them to take a break from each other for a while (in **The One Where Ross and Rachel Take a Break**). Her ultimatum drove Ross down to the neighbourhood bar, where he ended up drinking massive quantities of beer. And, later, he crawled into bed with Chloe, the sexy girl from the Xerox store.

Try as he might to cover his tracks the following day, Rachel found out the awful truth (in **The One the Morning After**).

The rift between Ross and Rachel threatened to break up the group (in **The One with the Ski Trip**). They were so bitter about the break-up that they couldn't even be in the same room together – which meant the rest of the gang could only hang out with one or the other. On one particular winter weekend, Ross ended up losing out to Rachel – when she lured everyone to Vermont to her sister's cabin for a ski weekend. Of course, when their car broke down on the interstate, it was Ross who rescued them, although they didn't tell Rachel they'd called him. "What is *he* doing here?" Rachel demanded when he pulled up at the rest stop where they were marooned. And, in a matter of seconds, the two had become embroiled in another "we were on a break" debate. They only let up

after Chandler had what looked like a seizure. (Actually, he was doing his impression of Shelley Winters in *The Poseidon Adventure*.) Phoebe told the battling couple that if they couldn't figure out a way to be around each other, it would inevitably lead to the end of the group. Guiltily (and reluctantly), Ross and Rachel agreed to a cessation of hostilities. With that, the others climbed into the car and headed back on to the interstate. But now it was Ross's turn to be stranded, because his car wouldn't start.

Phoebe continued her own unique brand of crisis counselling with her half-brother Frank Jr and his fiancée in **The One with the Hypnosis Tape**. It wasn't that she didn't like Mrs Knight, the woman Frank Jr wanted to marry, it was just that she was so much older than he was. In fact, she'd been his Home Ec. teacher in high school. Phoebe begged Joey and Ross to talk some sense into her brother. But Frank Jr was so happy and so much in love that they ended up having a group hug instead. Phoebe convinced Mrs Knight to break things off with Frank Jr, but he was so devastated that she had to bring her back over to explain why this was the best thing for both of them. Mrs Knight tried to make the speech the way Phoebe wanted her to, and she was doing pretty well, until she and Frank Jr (literally) fell into a passionate embrace.

Ross was sure that Rachel was going to beg him to come back when she asked him to come over in **The One with the Tiny T-Shirt**. All

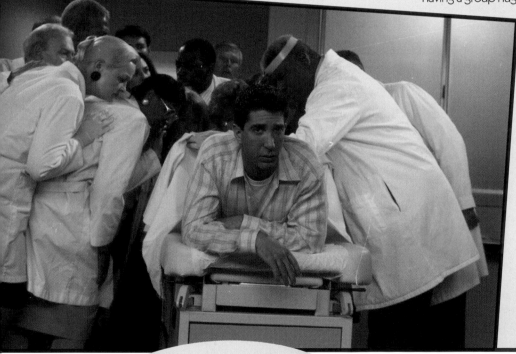

◀ The doctors have never seen anything like Ross's Thing.

"We had a bathtub duck and a walking duck," remembers Michael Lembeck, director of The One with the Chick and a Duck. "The walking duck was like a character actor – he always did funny stuff with his tail that made us laugh. We also had a stuffed chick that we used as a chick double. For the part where Chandler puts the chick in the tub to see if it can swim, we dammed up the tub and put it in a pail. There was a duck cam and a chick cam and we just kept rolling so we always had plenty of stuff."

Kate, Joey's beautiful co-star in a very bad off-off Broadway play, insisted that she didn't know why her character would be attracted to Joey's character. (Yeah, sure she didn't.)

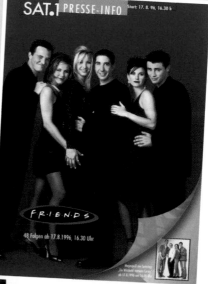

He's a merman! The gang played a little joke on Joey after he fell into a deep margarita-induced sleep at the beach house.

she wanted, though, was to return the junk he'd left at her place. Embarrassed, and angrier at Rachel than ever, he demanded that she also hand over his "Frankie Say Relax" T-shirt – even though he knew that Rachel loved to sleep in it. Meanwhile, Monica's romance with a guy named Pete Becker was starting to heat up. Now this guy Pete was seriously rich and crazy about Monica. She told Pete that she was at a place in her life where she wanted to focus on herself. OK, she backtracked, that was baloney. The truth was Monica just wasn't attracted to him. He predicted that she might end up changing her mind.

Ross was in for some high anxiety in **The One with Ross's Thing**. You see, he had this, uh, little growth on a part of his body that was not "visually accessible" to him. He asked Joey and Chandler to check it out, but they didn't know what it was. And even the doctors at the hospital had never seen anything like it. It took Phoebe's fruitcake herbalist, Guru Saj, to identify the whatsit as a coundis. He got the coundis to pop off, but unfortunately for Guru Saj, it caught on his watch.

The last episode of the third season (**The One at the Beach**), found everyone heading out to Montauk to stay at the beach house that belonged to Phoebe's massage client with the fuzzy back. While the others played, Phoebe set out to track down her mother's best friend from high school (also named Phoebe), who happened to live in the area. But Big Phoebe was surprisingly evasive. Phoebe, however, sneaked into her house to see if she could dig up any information – only to be caught by Big Phoebe who told her that *she was her real mother!*

Back at the beach house Rachel made big mischief by encouraging Ross's weekend date, the very cute Bonnie, to shave her head. When Ross pinned Rachel as the instigator of Bonnie's billiard-ball look, she admitted that maybe she still felt something for him. Before you could say "season finale", they found themselves locked together in an embrace – until Joey and Chandler interrupted them. Casting a meaningful eye in Ross's direction, Rachel announced that she was going to her bedroom. After agonizing over what to do, Ross made his way up the stairs, pausing first at Bonnie's door, then at Rachel's. Slowly he opened one and stepped inside.

Marta Kauffman, David Crane and director Peter Bonerz give notes to Matthew Perry and Courteney Cox as first assistant director Ben Weiss looks on on the set of The One with the Screamer.

SAT.1 PRESSE-INFO   Start: 17. 8. 96, 16.30 h

F·R·I·E·N·D·S

48 Folgen ab 17.8.1996, 16.30 Uhr

Friends is even funny in German.

LISA KUDROW PROFILE

A funny thing happened to Lisa Kudrow on her way to becoming a doctor after graduating from college … she became a star. Not that she wouldn't have been a star at anything she tried, mind you, including researching cluster headaches – her original interest. The thing is, you see, … she's not ditsy like Phoebe. In fact, she's really smart. *How* smart, you ask? Let's just say that her nickname at school was "Einstein" and leave it at that.

Lisa describes herself as "JAP-py" (as in Jewish American Princess), and it's true that she is a doctor's daughter who was born and raised in the heart of Valley Girl country – Encino, California, an upscale suburb of

"Lisa has her own quirky personality, but it's 180 degrees from Phoebe. In many ways she's the most settled of the show's cast."
– David Crane

Los Angeles. But despite the fact that she lived in the film capital of the world, Lisa wasn't one of those kids who sat around dreaming about becoming a movie star. No, the closest she got to performing as a child was throwing a rag over her head and lip-synching to the soundtrack of *Fiddler on the Roof* to amuse her schoolmates.

Lisa seemed destined to follow in the footsteps of her father, the eminent headache authority Dr Lee Kudrow. She was a bookworm in primary school, an A student throughout high school, and a pre-med, then biology major in college. Kudrow graduated from the prestigious Vassar College with a Bachelor of Science degree

Yes, they really are friends. Lisa Kudrow and Courteney Cox get the giggles during a rehearsal.

Over the years we've come to know a lot about Phoebe's family –
although not necessarily in the following order ...

Phoebe didn't know until the third year of *Friends* that her real
mother was Big Phoebe – who'd given her and her twin sister
Ursula up to Lily, soon after they were born. Lily was Big
Phoebe's best friend from high school. She'd also been a friend
of Phoebe's father, Frank Buffay – and, together with Lily, they
were known as "The Three Losers". Lily, Phoebe's adoptive
mother, committed suicide by putting her head in an (unlit) oven
– leaving Phoebe and Ursula to fend for themselves on the mean
city streets. Her stepfather couldn't help because he was a guest
of the state in an upstate prison. Her grandmother (Lily's mother),
with whom she sometimes lived, had told her that her birth-father
was the handsome guy in the photographs that came in picture
frames. But she eventually admitted that he was really a pharmacist
in upstate New York. When Phoebe drove there to confront him, she
found that he had abandoned his second family, too. However, she
met and became close to her half-brother, Frank Jr, and eventually
gestates his (and his wife Alice's) triplets. She had a brief talk with
Frank Sr after her grandmother died, but he quickly fled once he
realized who she was. And that's where we left things at the end
of the fifth year.

in 1985, fully intending to pursue her interest in medicine – which was driven by the family's genetic
predisposition towards migraines. It was her father's
own cluster headaches – painful attacks that occur
in series – that had sparked his research initially.
But then, in 1985, the year that Lisa graduated
from college, her brother's close friend, the
comic Jon Lovitz, landed a spot on *Saturday
Night Live*. Lovitz's new job impressed Lisa,
and awakened acting ambitions until then
buried deep inside her. "I don't know
how I could have come back to L.A. and
not been an actor," she says now. "It's
too much. It's in the air."

Lovitz recommended that
Lisa audition for The Groundlings,
the Los Angeles improvisational
comedy troupe that had sharp-
ened his talents as well as those
of Paul Reubens (Pee Wee
Herman) and Laraine Newman
among others. Lisa began
studying with Cynthia Szigeti,

Phoebe went back to singing on the street after she was fired from Central Perk, but after almost a full day, she had only earned 8 dollars and 27 cents – and not really even that, as she had put in the first two dollars herself. Here Rachel tries to cheer her up with a cup of mocha java.

an improvisation teacher in Los Angeles and by 1989 she was performing with The Groundlings' A-team improv group in its West Hollywood theatre.

During the troupe's weekly shows she developed a number of characters that won her a kind of cult following – most notably a bumbling doctor-type who lectured in incomprehensible medicalese. Within a few years Lisa was a well-known member of the Los Angeles comedy scene, one who spent her nights performing and her days auditioning for sitcom and movie guest shots. She won a few small parts in low-budget movies,

and a role in a local theatre production called *The Ladies Room*. Her first TV job of note was the role of the girlfriend of Woody Harrelson's character on an episode of *Cheers*. Similar brief spells on *Coach* and *Newhart* followed, but it was 1993 before she finally landed the breakthrough role of Ursula on *Mad About You*. Her hilarious comedic turns as the warped waitress were a hit not only with audiences but also with the NBC brass, who encouraged her to audition for some of its sitcom pilots. One of those auditions led to her being cast briefly as Roz on *Frasier* – only to be replaced at the last

"When you write lines for a character," says David Crane, "you always hear them in your head – but Lisa will always find something you could never have imagined."

Phoebe Buffay wouldn't be caught dead in jeans or T-shirts, but her clothes are anything but traditional. She has always tended towards long, flowing dresses with psychedelic or flowery prints - sixties-era stuff found in thrift shops. While still zany and more or less in the same vein, Phoebe's clothes became sexier and more revealing in the fifth year of *Friends*.

"Hello, this is Ross Geller's personal physician, Dr Falangie. I discovered that Ross forgot to take his brain medicine. Now, without it, in the brain of Ross, women's names are interchangeable through no fault of his own." - Phoebe explaining Ross's wedding vow gaffe to his new mother-in-law

minute by Peri Gilpin. Happily, the network was set on providing a vehicle for Lisa Kudrow's unique talents, and it wasn't long before she was cast in *Friends*.

In an unusual twist, Lisa continued to play Ursula on *Mad About You* while at the same time playing Phoebe – whom the *Friends* producers deftly birthed as Ursula's twin sister. Eventually Ursula herself would make an appearance on *Friends*, where she had a little fling with Joey during the first season, and then again a year later when she became the object of an inept stalker who kept confusing her with Phoebe. When Ursula appears

with Phoebe during her occasional visits, Lisa Kudrow's sister, artist Helene Sherman, serves as a double for over-the-shoulder shots.

You could say that Lisa Kudrow is the Friend with the most experience in what is sometimes referred to as the Real World. Until Courteney Cox's recent marriage, she was the only married member of the cast. Her husband is French advertising executive Michel Stern, and, for now, she remains the only parental Friend – having given birth to a son, Julian, in 1998.

Lisa Kudrow says that she is someone who's "never been good at relaxing", and she proved that by managing to work in several film roles during each *Friends* summer hiatus. She starred opposite Mira Sorvino in the uproarious comedy *Romy & Michele's High School Reunion*. She had small but super-cool parts in *Mother* with Albert Brooks and *Analyze This* with Billy Crystal and Robert DeNiro. During the fourth season's summer break, she starred with Christina Ricci, Lyle Lovett and Martin Donovan as a repressed schoolteacher with a biting wit in *The Opposite of Sex*. Her engaging performance in that film won her nominations for several awards, among them the New York Film Critics Award – which she took home.

Speaking of awards, in 1995, 1997 and 1998 Lisa won Emmy nominations for Outstanding Supporting Actress in a Comedy Series for her work on *Friends*. To her fans' delight, she finally won the Emmy in that category in September 1998, making her the most critically lauded member of the *Friends* cast (for now, anyway). As Matt LeBlanc warned everyone when Lisa fell into a giggling fit during a rehearsal, "Watch out ... when she gets like this, she starts farting awards."

To her fans' delight, Lisa Kudrow won the Emmy for Outstanding Supporting Actress in a Comedy Series in September of 1998, making her (for now) the most critically lauded member of the *Friends* cast.

Photo by Criag T. Mathew

We know that four of the Friends have known each other since their college days, but the origin of Monica and Ross's close friendship with Phoebe is still something of a mystery. A quick bit of maths would have Phoebe still living on the street at the time they all met. Soon after that she became Monica's roommate for a brief time. Had the soft-hearted Monica taken pity on Phoebe and taken her in? Whatever the case, she didn't stay with her long. She moved on to her grandmother's place - and that's where she was living when we first met her.

THE FRIENDS' DATING GAME

Compared to the rest of her sex-obsessed friends, Phoebe sometimes comes across as being almost oblivious to the opposite sex – anyway that's the way it sometimes seemed during the show's first few episodes.

Not until **The One with the Monkey** did we see Phoebe with her very own Boy Toy. Unfortunately, though, her new love interest, **David** – a physicist and a pussycat, if there ever was one – got a hot work opportunity in Minsk.

Phoebe's next boyfriend was **Roger**, the obnoxious shrink, who was constantly analysing the group and then making annoyingly accurate assessments about their neurotic interdependence. Eventually Phoebe had to tell Roger that her friends had a "liking problem" with him.

In **The One after the Superbowl**, Phoebe took up with a really cute guy named **Rob** (guest star Chris Isaak) who liked her music so much that he wanted her to sing for his children's group at the library. The kids liked her songs, too – especially the one about how their parents had lied when they said grandma had gone to Peru … "But the truth is she died, and some day you will, too."

"The studio audience loved Charlie Sheen," says Michael Lembeck, who directed the film star in The One with the Chicken Pox, "and that was great because he was scared to death to do a live shoot. His brother, Emilio Estevez, stayed with him on the stage to give him support. As the night went on, Charlie got looser and funnier and the laughs came faster and easier. By the end of the shoot, he was a total pro."

▲ Guest star Chris Isaak joins Phoebe in a chorus of "Smelly Cat" in The One After the Superbowl.

The better we got to know her, the more we realized that Phoebe was surprisingly open-minded about sex. In **The One with the Chicken Pox**, she revealed that she spent a deeply romantic no-strings weekend with a dishy naval officer named **Ryan** (guest star Charlie Sheen) when he and his submarine came up for air every other year. Then there was the super-cool way she dealt with her sexually stand-offish boyfriend, **Scott**. He had this concern (he said) about ruining their relationship by getting too (physically) involved. Whew … was Phoebe relieved! She'd been afraid that she didn't turn him on. Just "relax and enjoy it", Phoebe told him. (Joey was impressed: "You mean to tell me that he got you to *beg* to sleep with *him*? This man is my *god!*")

Let's face it: Phoebe's boyfriends are as kooky as she is. Take the preppy-looking "J. Crew Guy" named **Malcolm** (guest star David Arquette) who followed her all over town for days in **The One with the Jam**. Yes, he was a stalker – and an inept one, at that, as his stalkee was supposed to have been Ursula,

▲ Call her crazy, but Phoebe thought her stalker, Malcolm (guest star David Arquette), was really cute.

Phoebe's twin sister. He promised Phoebe that he was over Ursula and crazy for her, but when she followed him to see whether he'd really reformed, she found him lurking behind a pillar at Ursula's subway stop. Phoebe told him gently that she couldn't date him any more because he was, like, you know … insane.

Phoebe's next squeeze, **Robert** (from **The One Where Monica and Richard are Friends**), was a really sweet guy, but he kept coming out of his shorts – or as Chandler so delicately put it, "The man is showing brain!"

▲ Joey and Chandler got to see a lot more of Robert than they bargained for!

Then in **The One Where Ross and Rachel Take a Break**, she met a dashing Central Asian diplomat named **Sergei** while giving free massages at the UN. (The way she figured it, bodies at peace *make* peace.) The problem was that Sergei didn't speak any English and every time things started to get interesting between them, his translator got in the way.

Phoebe was on a roll in **The One with Ross's Thing**. She was dating two very cute guys at the same time. One was Vince, a hunky fireman who had 98 hot saves and was super-serious about fire safety. The other was Jason, a kind-hearted kindergarten teacher who was extremely good-looking. "I'm playing the field," she told the others exultantly. "I'm juggling two guys. I'm sowing my wild oats. I'm like some kind of oat-sowing, field-playing juggler!" But one night at Central Perk while Vince was watching her sing ("Crazy Underwear Creeping Up My Butt"), Jason walked in and kissed her (on the lips). Ultimately, Jason walked out because she had slept with

▲ Phoebe brought Monica along on a date with her diplomat boyfriend so as to keep his translator occupied, but the two of them got along so well together, she and Sergei were left with nothing to say.

Vince; and Vince cut her loose because she'd made Jason a candlelit dinner in the park. There was no way, he told her sorrowfully, that he could be serious about someone who would light a fire in a wooded area.

In **The One with the Ballroom Dancing** Phoebe found herself attracted to one of her massage clients – a violation of her masseuse's oath (which she had made up herself). But this guy **Rick** was so adorable that she found herself wanting to do things to him that she couldn't charge for. But then, in a moment of reckless abandon, she suddenly bent over and bit his tushy. Unable to hold back any longer, she told Rick how she felt, and the two of them started kissing. Her boss *would* pick that moment to do a walk-through with another client. Phoebe, doing some fast thinking, said that things weren't the way they appeared – that, in fact, she and Rick were, that's right, married. That was interesting, her boss observed

Rick was a client, so Phoebe couldn't tell him that she had The Feelings for him. Instead, she let her tarted-up toes do the talking – which made sense seeing as they were the only part of her body he could see when he was lying on her table.

drily, since his other wife had called three times that day looking for him.

Before long, Phoebe had fallen for a gung-ho health inspector (in **The One Where Ross Moves In**). She loved it when Larry flashed his badge, and she also loved to go out to dinner with him, because he knew all the clean places to eat in. But, darn it, this guy kept closing down all her favourite restaurants. Phoebe told him that if he just *had* to bust someone that night, she knew a hot dog vendor who picked his nose.

Phoebe found an NYPD badge of her own (in **The One with the Cop**), and she had a great time using it to bust people for doing environmentally incorrect misdeeds – like the woman who put her cigarette out on a tree while Phoebe was watching. Along with the badge came a new boyfriend named **Gary**, a real NYPD cop who thought Phoebe was funny – especially when she told him she was an undercover hooker from the vice squad. He told her she was the prettiest fake

◀ At first Phoebe enjoyed playing the field by dating two very cute guys at the same time. But keeping up the deception began to make her feel as if she was working in the field. It wasn't long before the inevitable happened.

▶ Phoebe loved it when Larry the Health Inspector guy flashed his badge.

undercover whore he'd ever seen and he let her ride with him in his squad car in **The One with the Ride-along.**

Gary told Phoebe (in **The One with the Ball**) that he wanted her to move in with him. But Phoebe had this nagging suspicion that something wasn't right between them. The mystery was solved several nights later when she slept over at Gary's apartment for the first time. They woke up to the lovely sound of a chirping songbird outside the window, and then Gary picked up his revolver and shot it dead. Bye-bye Gary.

~

For the most part, **Joey**'s *affaires d'amour* tend to be a little more casual than those of the rest of the gang. Tellingly, perhaps, Joey's first serious romance came (literally) in the form of Phoebe in **The One with Two Parts, Part 1.** Not with Phoebe herself, but with her identical twin sister, **Ursula** – the spacey waitress who normally inhabits the parallel sitcom world of *Mad About You.* But Phoebe was anything but flattered by Joey's infatuation with her lookalike. No, the whole situation made her extremely uncomfortable. To begin with, she and Ursula were estranged – and that made things awkward for both her and the gang. And, more importantly, she was worried for Joey – what with Ursula being a total bitch and all.

Joey is for sure a babe-magnet, but he's had his share of oddball romances. In **The One Where Mr Heckles Dies**, Joey reminisced about a little fling he'd had with a girl with a giant Adam's apple (translation: a man). And then there was **Ginger,** the girl whose artificial leg he threw into the fireplace. But we had never seen Joey truly in love until he met **Kate** while working in an off-off-Broadway play (in **The One with the Tiny**

Lauren, Kate's perky blonde understudy, was in awe of Joey and his impressive body of work as Dr Drake Ramoray in *Days of Our Lives.*

▲ Kate left New York for a job on a soap opera in L.A. But at least she stopped by the theatre to say goodbye to Joey (almost making him miss his entrance). Maybe she really did care about him after all.

T-Shirt). Not that Kate thought much of him – at first, anyway. During rehearsals (in **The One with the Dollhouse**) she complained that she didn't see why her character would be attracted to someone like Joey, but after he melted her with a passionate kiss, she understood just fine. Joey lost no time making his move, but Kate hung tight with her boyfriend, the play's crackpot director, as ever. Kate's interest in Joey perked up after she overheard him making a date with Lauren, her understudy. But even though she eventually slept with him, she acted as if nothing had changed between them the next day when they were at rehearsal. What was the deal, he demanded. He knew their night together had meant *something* to her, he told her. She wasn't *that* good an actress. And neither was he, apparently. His reviews (in **The One With the Screamer**) were terrible, but so were Kate's. In a sweet effort to

console her afterwards at the opening-night party, Joey assured her the critics were just jealous because she was so darn talented and good-looking. She felt better and started to nuzzle him. "I don't get you," he told her, "first you hate me, then you sleep with me, then you have nothing to do with me. Now you want me again?" "What's the matter?" she asked innocently. "Haven't you ever dated an actress before?" Before he could answer, she had passed out. Joey was still with her when she woke up at home later. And they ended up talking till daybreak – a first for both of them. But the following night, when Joey made his first entrance in the next play, Kate had gone and Lauren was playing her part. Kate had got a job on *General Hospital,* and she was off to L.A. that night, but she did take a minute to stop by the theatre to say good-bye.

Joey wasn't all that eager to get romantically involved with anyone after what he'd gone through with Kate – although he was always open to getting something going with Monica or Rachel (or, failing that, getting something going *between* Monica and Rachel). He even started having impure thoughts about Monica after things started to heat up between her and Chandler. But he would have to be content with his fantasies until the following season.

When Monica told Joey that the reason she and Chandler were so compatible was that they had been friends before they were lovers, Joey took it to mean that he should put the make on Rachel.

~

Was it always there … that little romantic spark between **Chandler** and **Monica**? We knew that they'd shared some intimate moments – like when Chandler peed on her legs (for medicinal purposes). And then there were those little "what if?" scenarios he was always concocting – like when he suggested to Monica that they should have a child together if they were still single at 40.

What we didn't know until the fifth season of *Friends* was that Monica had had a crush on Chandler years ago – back when Ross first brought him home from college for a Thanksgiving weekend. But Chandler had told Ross that he didn't want to get stuck with his "fat sister". As much as it hurt, Chandler's comment about her weight problem changed Monica's life for the better.

When Chandler visited again the following year, he was awestruck at

▶

This is where it all started. Monica got a huge crush on Chandler when Ross brought him home from college for the Thanksgiving holiday. But Chandler told Ross that he didn't want to get stuck with his "fat sister".

the sight of the new, streamlined Monica. But Monica wanted more. She wanted to humiliate Chandler as he'd humiliated her. She would entice him into thinking that she would make out with him, and then get him to take off his clothes. Next she would throw him through the door for all the neighbours to see. But if she was going to seduce Chandler she would do it right there in the kitchen while no one was looking. Grabbing a tea-towel, Rachel proceeded to show her how to be sexy with kitchen implements – caressing her cheek with the towel and purring about how oh-so-good it felt against her skin. But Monica's version of this kitchen come-on ended up being predictably manic. She started with a box of macaroni cheese, which she rubbed against her cheek. Then she added a bunch of carrots and a huge carving knife in her other hand. It was tricky holding on to all this stuff, let alone rubbing it over her body, and talking about how sexy it made her feel. It was so tricky,

▲ Was it there all along...that little spark between Chandler and Monica?

in fact, that she ended up flipping the carving knife into the air. It landed on poor Chandler's foot and severed his toe.

~

But we're getting ahead of ourselves. Before we take a look at the union of prime time's two most endearing neurotics, let's do a little reminiscing about who – and what – both Monica and Chandler finally had to go through to make it into each other's arms.

~

That **Monica** could pick 'em, couldn't she? From **Julio** the full-of-it bus boy to **Ethan** the high school senior, her track record for picking boyfriends has been pathetically bad. And it wasn't as if she didn't know it. "Is it me?" she once said. "Is it like I have some sort of beacon that only dogs and men with severe emotional problems can hear?" The way Monica saw it, she was continually falling for Mr Wrong. In the very first episode Monica allowed herself to be seduced by a wine salesman named **Paul** who told her how he hadn't been able to perform sexually since his wife had left him two years ago. It was only a matter of days before Monica discovered that her co-worker Franny had also ministered to Paul in his time of need.

▲ Monica is crying over Old Yeller now, but she'll be crying over her break-up with Richard in just a few episodes.

Monica's perpetual man-trouble was particularly excruciating because her search for the right guy was rooted in a serious longing: she really (really) wants to get married and start a family. Now that doesn't mean she's a prude – or that she doesn't allow herself the sexual perks of singlehood now and then. In fact, she can be pretty kinky, darn it. Take the time back in college when she had sex on a pool table … and then there was that hickey she got from one of the Blowfish (of Hootie and the …). And what about the time she played Dirty Old Lady with a guy who was still in high school?

Sometimes it seems that Monica's biggest turn-off is the Totally Suitable Guy Who Actually Likes Her. Witness **Alan** (from **The One with the Thumb**): he was crazy about her, and he was so cool that even her fussy friends approved of him. The problem was that Monica didn't. (Which turned out to be sort of OK, since Alan didn't like her friends.)

Next came the legendary **Fun Bobby**. Everyone got happy when Fun Bobby was around – including Monica. There was just one little drawback: Fun

▶ Tom Selleck (the real Tom) says that he was overcome with jealousy the first time he saw (his TV lover) Monica dating someone else on Friends.

90

▶

Monica thinks Julio could be just the thing to help her get over Richard. But Julio thinks she's nothing more than a beautiful but "empty vase".

Bobby was only fun when he was drinking. And he drank, as Rachel pointed out to Monica in **The One with Russ**, practically all the time. After a serious heart-to-heart with Monica, Bobby agreed to go on the wagon. But when Fun Bobby was sober, he was so boring that he drove Monica to take up drinking herself.

Wouldn't you know that when Monica finally did find her Mr Right, he would turn out to be old enough to be her father. Moreover, as (bad) luck would have it, **Dr Richard Burke** was actually an old friend of her parents who'd known her since she was small enough to pee in his pool. But, hey, the guy looked like Tom Selleck. (In fact, he *was* Tom Selleck.)

The grown-up Monica got reacquainted with Dr Burke (in **The One Where Ross and Rachel … You Know**) when he hired her to cook for a party. He had just split up with his wife of 30 years, and the party was meant to signal his return into the social scene. But Dr Burke's guests didn't interest him nearly as much as his lovely caterer. He was clearly smitten – and he didn't try to hide it. Shaky about getting involved with her parents' friend, Monica nevertheless agreed to go out with the doctor. Back in her apartment after their trial date, the irksome reality of the situation came into focus as they looked at photos of Richard's daughter and grandchild. "Are we nuts here?" he suddenly asked her. "This really sucks," Monica agreed. But then he took her in his arms and said, "We don't have to decide anything now, do we?".

Not only was the physical relationship between Monica and Richard incredibly juicy, but the two of them had fallen truly, madly, deeply in love. There was no way to keep a lid on something that hot, and, sure enough, it wasn't long before word of Richard's affair had travelled back to Monica's mother. All she knew, she told a friend as Monica squirmed uneasily, was that Richard had a "twenty-year-old Twinkie in the city". She went predictably ballistic when she found out that the Twinkie was none other than her darling daughter.

Monica and Richard didn't need the Gellers to point out the inequity of their age difference. The issue popped up in all sorts of unexpected areas. The mere idea that Monica had had sex with as many men as she had done was totally unnerving for Richard. His hit list was considerably smaller, confined as it was to his wife of 30 years – and now Monica. Then there was the necessity for protected sex, which first came up (in **The One Where Dr Ramoray Dies**) when Monica lost out to Rachel in a battle for the last condom. "They're doing it tonight," she told Richard as she stomped past him into her bedroom. "We'll do it tomorrow."

Sad to say, Monica herself couldn't get past the obstacle of Richard's age – a realization that dawned on her in **The One with Barry and Mindy's Wedding**. He was so perfect … in so many ways. It was just that he didn't want to have children. Not that he didn't like them. He loved them. He *had* them. Grown ones. Of course, Monica wanted kids more than anything in the world. "If I have to," Richard told her half-heartedly, "I'll do it again." But Monica, straight-shooter that she is, just couldn't ask for that kind of sacrifice from him.

Their subsequent break-up was so shattering for Monica that she literally couldn't sleep or eat. She even found herself collecting Richard's plughole hair (in **The One with the Princess Leia Fantasy**). Yeah, it was gross, but it was practically all she had left of him. (Or rather, it was until she dropped it into Ross's cereal bowl.)

Still torching for Richard in the following season, Monica had taken a job as a singing short-order cook in a 1950s theme restaurant. She was so pessimistic (in **The One with the Jam**) about her prospects for marriage that she'd begun considering making a withdrawal from a sperm bank. But on the day she was leaving for the sperm bank Joey happened to ask her what the guy she'd picked was like. "Dark hair, green eyes," she answered. Funny, Joey said, he'd always imagined her with a blond guy, with a swimmer's body and a name like Hoyt. In fact, the picture of her and her husband and their children was so real to him that he could actually see it. And by the time he had finished, Monica could see it, too.

Then (in **The One with All the Jealousy**) along came Julio, a dishy but egotistical bus boy from the diner, who seduced her and then wrote a bitchy little poem describing her as a beautiful but "empty vase". This was the perfect time for Richard to reappear in her life. They tried to stay just "platonic" friends, but that didn't last long. Monica had an idea … why couldn't they be friends who slept together? Richard was game. But when she tried to surprise him with an unannounced visit to his apartment, she was horrified to hear him come in with a date. Luckily Richard realized that she was hiding under the covers in his bedroom, so she didn't get caught. Getting over him was the hardest thing she'd ever gone through, she told Richard, and she realized now

that she couldn't go through it again. OK, so they were over, he acknowledged. But that didn't mean that they had to start that night.

By **The One with the Hypnosis Tape**, Monica had gone so long without a date that she started lobbying Rachel to fix her up with someone. Overhearing their conversation, **Pete Becker** decided to take his shot. This Pete was a good guy … and a rich one, too. And he was totally in love with Monica. To prove it, he bought her a big, fancy restaurant of her own (in **The One with the Chick and the Duck**). But as sweet and as cuddly as he was, Pete also turned out to be pretty far out there, too – which Monica realized once she

▲ "We always knew we wanted Monica to get involved with a Bill Gates billionaire genius scientist-type whom she wasn't physically attracted to in any way," says David Crane. "But it was very tough casting thing because you had to have someone who was appealing enough that we liked him, so we could root for him, but on the other hand, wasn't so drop-dead male model gorgeous that we would go, 'What's your problem?' to Monica when she didn't fall for him."

found out about his obsession with winning the brutal Ultimate Fighting competition. After he was beaten to a pulp in his second fight (in **The One with the Ultimate Fighting Champion**), Monica gave him an ulti-matum: it was either her or this death-wish warrior trip, she told him, as he lay in the locker room. Pete chose the death-wish warrior trip.

At least Monica kept moving – although in the wrong direction in the case of **Chip Matthews**, a guy she'd known since high school. She couldn't help but be thrilled when he asked her out (in **The One with the Cat**); he had been the most popular boy in school while she had been a chubby no-hoper. A date with Chip meant

"The truth of the matter is, kissing a pretty actress is not a romantic or sexy situation. It's all angles and lights. It's all technical ... 'Move your shoulder here'. There are 50 people watching, boom operators, script supervisors. It's not a sexy thing." — Matthew Perry on how he avoids becoming aroused during a kissing scene

that she had finally made it. But appar-ently Chip had been so comfortable in high school that he had never left it: he still worked at the local Cineplex, lived with his parents, and drove the same souped-up motorcycle. And the only thing he talked about was the old gang and the Old Days.

Despite her best intentions, the next place Monica landed was on **Tim Burke**, Richard's son. Not that she meant to. It was just one of those (Monica) things. She tried to act as if things were perfectly normal when Tim joined her and the gang for Thanksgiving dinner. But, later, as they stood on the balcony together, she told him that her friends all thought that the idea of the two of them together was creepy. He answered by kissing

...so began the tumultuous secret affair between Chandler and Monica that has been the source of so much inspired lunacy during the fifth year of *Friends*.

In that season Chandler Bing found the love of his life living right across the hall. For most of the four years before, however, he had been entangled with the deeply annoying **Janice** – although he'd spent almost all of that time trying to get rid of her. And it's not hard to understand why: she's shallow and needy and she whinnies when she laughs.

It's not as though Chandler was all that tolerant of female imperfection to begin with. If you remember, he broke up with the totally nice **Joan** from work simply because her nostrils were too big. (He said that bats flew out of her nose when she sneezed.) The exotic and worldly **Aurora** passed Chandler's suitability test with flying colours (in **The One with the Butt**). Unlike Janice, she was strong and independent and totally loose about sex. Aurora thought Chandler was pretty nifty, too. Almost as nifty as her husband and her other boyfriend (and the new boyfriend whom she picked up during her affair with Chandler).

Chandler's dream encounter with supermodel **Jill Goodacre** (playing herself) turned into a disaster when they were trapped together in an ATM vestibule during a power cut (in **The One with the Blackout**). Paralysed by the idea of occupying the same air space, Chandler choked on a stick of gum that Goodacre offered him. After the power returned, Chandler got a kiss from Jill and a surveillance-camera video to commemorate their

her. But she didn't react well. Was that not OK, he asked. "No," she said quickly, "that was a gooooood kiss." What had freaked her out was that the kiss reminded her so much of his father.

Imagine Monica's state of mind by the time Ross's wedding rolled around. By this point, she'd been through one romantic fiasco after another. And now her big brother was getting married for the second time, and not only was there no one special in her life, she didn't even have a date. Monica's troubles escalated from the minute everyone arrived in London. Ross blamed her for talking Emily out of the wedding – and in a way, she had. Her mother was on her case as usual and everyone was fighting – Ross and Emily, Chandler and Joey, and even the Gellers and the Walthams – who almost came to blows over who was going to pay for what. Then Phoebe started calling frantically to say that Rachel was on her way over to ruin the wedding. No wonder Monica got plastered on the night of the rehearsal dinner. But she still might have made it back to her own room – and bed – alone if one of the guests hadn't mistaken her for Ross's mother. "My mom's right," she moaned to Chandler. "I'm never going to get married." But Chandler told her that was ridiculous. "Who *wouldn't* want you?" he said passionately.

The next time we saw the two of them, it was the following morning and they were in bed together. And

Must've been that last blow to the head: when Monica told Pete he would have to choose between a blissful life with her and debilitating pain, he chose pain.

special evening together. But kiss or no kiss, he was pretty sure that Jill Goodacre thought he was a geek.

What kind of strange signals was he giving out anyway? He had to wonder when his co-worker Shelly tried to fix him up with a guy from the office. And then Monica and Rachel told him that they'd thought he had a certain "quality" too, when they first met him. But while he insisted that he was straight, it should be duly noted that Chandler's most memorable kiss of the whole first season was delivered by Joey in **The One with the Monkey**. (It was New Year's Eve and Chandler had been adamant that *somebody* kiss him.)

Things always went wrong for Chandler on holidays. On Valentine's Day Joey lined him up with a blind date (in **The One with the Candy Hearts**) and – just his luck – it turned out to be Janice. Chandler handled the situation by getting drunk and having sex with her – only to break up with her again the next morning. But she wasn't giving up. Later she brought him a custom-made candy heart that said "Chan and Jan 4 ever",

Susie (guest star Julia Roberts) avenged an old grudge she'd had against Chandler since grade school by sweet-talking him into slipping into her tiny pink thong, and then luring him into the men's room of a fancy restaurant. She then sneaked out with his clothes — leaving him to make his exit from the place with nothing but the detached stall door to cover his embarrassment.

and told him, "You don't know it yet, but you love me, Chandler Bing."

Janice would put in a surprise appearance in **The One Where Mr Heckles Dies** when Chandler – positive that he was going to end up a friendless, crabby old man like the late Mr Heckles – called and begged her to come back. But the next day, when she walked into Central Perk, it was clear that she was very pregnant. "You *wish*, Chandler Bing," she whooped when he timorously asked whether the baby was his. But Janice said no … she had married "The Mattress King", a local celeb who sold discount beds on TV. "You couldn't have told me about this over the phone?" he asked her. "What, and miss your face?" she answered. "Oh no, Janice likes to have her fun."

At last Chandler was free – free from Janice, and free to do the whole bachelor bit. And he would have done, if only he weren't so incredibly bad at it. Take the time (in **The One with Five Steaks and an Eggplant**) when he happened to intercept a wrong-number call

from a really sexy-sounding girl named **Jade** who was trying to track down an old boyfriend named Bob. After making a date to meet her at Central Perk in the guise of this Bob, he actually managed to get her into bed (as himself). The next day found a seriously-pleased-with-himself Chandler bragging to Ross that he had been so awesome with this sexy Jade that she'd had to keep biting her lip to keep from screaming. As if on cue, Jade called Chandler's answering machine again to tell "Bob" that she had met a new guy two hours earlier and had even had sex with him – but that she'd had to bite her lip to keep from calling out Bob's name.

Chandler's next *liaison dangereuse* was **Susie** (guest star Julia Roberts). Although Chandler didn't

remember Susie at first, she reminded him that they had gone to grade school together, and that he had once pulled up her skirt during a school play – causing her to be known for ever afterwards as "Susie Underpants".

Chandler could hardly believe it, but this sexy Susie Underpants Person started coming on to him big time. Talking dirty. Telling him all the naughty things she wanted to do with (and to) him. But surprise, surprise … all Susie wanted to do was humiliate him the way he had humiliated her.

Fed up with flesh-and-blood females, Chandler retreated to the relatively tamer domain of cyber space in **The One with Barry and Mindy's Wedding**. But before you could say "You've got mail", he was having a torrid

on-line romance with a fabulous mystery woman. To check out his cyber-squeeze's gender, Chandler posed a few gender-specific questions – like what method of birth control she – or he – used. "My husband is sleeping with his secretary," was the prompt response. His pen pal was a woman all right. A married one. But Phoebe convinced him to go ahead and meet her in person. Chandler was an absolute basket-case while he awaited her arrival the next day at Central Perk. And with good reason, as it turned out. Because the mysterious Lady X turned out to be none other than Janice.

In **The One with the Metaphorical Tunnel**, Chandler vowed that if it was the last thing he did, he was going to get through that long, long tunnel with commitment on the other side. He even made a place (OK, a drawer) for Janice to keep her things in his apartment, but then it was Janice's turn to get cold feet. Here she was with her very own drawer in Chandler's apartment, and she hadn't even got a divorce from the Mattress

▲ Chandler: "Well, it's official, there are no good movies."
Janice: "Let's go to a bad one and make out." — Monica is more than just a little turned off as Janice makes the moves on Chandler at Central Perk. She offers to turn her back so they can bunny bump against her in The One with the Metaphorical Tunnel.

▶ "There was a moment [in The One with the Giant Poking Device]," says Maggie Wheeler, "when I'm hyperventilating into a paper bag because I'm so upset about leaving Chandler. Matthew was supposed to reach out and take it away from me, but he grabbed it with such force that it popped in my face. If you look at it on the finished show, you see that he's about to lose it, and I'm about to lose it. By the grace of God, I had the bag to hide in, and I just buried my head in it."

King yet. Not only that she'd been secretly double-timing Chandler.

Joey saved Janice the trouble of telling Chandler the truth after he caught her and her ex kissing in **The One with the Race Car Bed**. Chandler was suitably aghast. When he confronted Janice with her duplicity in **The One with the Giant Poking Device**, she became so agitated that it looked as if she was going to faint or throw up. The truth, she stammered, was that she loved both him and her ex. Chandler was devastated. Not just about Janice, but about the now-totally useless twelve-pack of condoms he'd bought that morning. After agonizing over the situation, he told her that he couldn't be responsible for breaking up a family – especially not after what he'd gone through with his own parents' divorce. Janice told him she knew he was right, and yet, "What we have," she said, "it's like movie love. You're my soul mate. And I can't believe we're not going to be spending the rest of our lives together." At this, Chandler's noble intentions flew right out of the window. "Then pick *me*," he sobbed, crumpling to the floor of the coffee house and wrapping himself around her legs to keep her from leaving. He even tried stealing one of her shoes. But it was too late. She hobbled out of his life (for now).

Chandler handled himself like a pro (in **The One with the Football**) with a slick-looking Dutch girl named **Margha**. In fact, he was so cool that Margha picked him over Joey – a first in the annals of Chandler. Crazy with joy, Chandler began to dance around Joey, chanting, "I win. You suck. I rule all. Mini-wave in celebration of me." As you might imagine, this performance didn't go

down well with Miss Holland. She quickly pronounced him shallow, and – how you say? – a dork.

For his next trick (in **The One Where Chandler Can't Remember**), Chandler got hammered on Jell-O shots at Joey's birthday party and ended up fooling around with one of Joey's sisters, **Angela**, in a storage room. The problem was that he couldn't remember which sister Angela was. And that was bad because there were seven of them. And they all looked alike. And they could all beat him to a pulp with one arm tied behind their backs – but Joey vetoed that plan on the condition that Chandler apologize. And he would have, too, if he only knew which sister was which.

Chandler and the luscious Ginger met outside the men's room at Central Perk in **The One with Phoebe's Ex-Partner**. They started dating, until Chandler discovered that Ginger had once had a thing with Joey – that is, she had until Joey threw her artificial leg into the fireplace while she was sleeping. Wait a minute ... *artificial leg*? Chandler was more than a little put off. But the next night, as he and Ginger were starting to get intimate, she got a gander at his third nipple, and was so repulsed that she ended up running away from *him*.

In **The One with the Dollhouse**, Chandler had another problem – the gross glob of mascara in the corner of Joanna's eye. **Joanna** was Rachel's incredibly bossy boss, whom Chandler had taken out once as a favour to Rachel. Chandler was definitely underwhelmed by their date, while Joanna just knew that the two of them had "clicked" like crazy. She pressured Rachel to get Chandler to call her back – as he had said he would. "I'm sorry I said I

▲
"Oh god, it freaked me out! I mean, I know it shouldn't have, but it did! I like her a lot. And I don't want to stop seeing her. But it's like – hey – where's your leg?" – Chandler

Chandler may have thought Joanna was a "big, dull dud" when he first went out with her, but that was before she played "The Boss" with him in his bedroom.

was going to call you when I'm not," Chandler told Joanna the next day. "This has nothing to do with you. I have issues with commitment, intimacy ... mascara goop."

Joanna showed up in Chandler's bedroom again in the fourth season (in **The One with the Cuffs**). Yes, there may have been a time when Chandler thought Joanna was a "big, dull dud", but that was before she played "The Boss" with him in his bedroom. Angrily, Rachel once again demanded that Chandler find someone else to boss him around. Her job was at stake, she told him, her security, her very future. Chandler got what she was saying and he would gladly have complied – if Joanna hadn't taken the bad news so darn well. The next time Rachel

saw Chandler, he was pantless and handcuffed to a chair in Joanna's office.

Chandler went on to develop a terrible crush on a girl Joey was dating. Her name was **Kathy**, and she was an actress. Chandler tried to tell Joey what he was feeling, but he was so wrought-up that Joey didn't believe him. Not that losing Kathy was all that big a deal to Joey. In fact, he already had his eye on another girl. What killed him was that Chandler had gone behind his back. No, he hadn't slept with her. But he *had* kissed her and he *did* love her and he hadn't told Joey – *his best friend*.

◄ When Rachel delicately suggested to Joanna that Chandler might feel awkward about dating her because she was her boss, Joanna replied pointedly that Rachel should be the one concerned about that.

pointed out that there wasn't always that much "agreement" the first time. But Chandler was panicked, and he begged for their help. Monica launched into an analysis of female sexuality with a complicated diagram of the seven erogenous zones. "The important thing is to take your time," she told him, "and hit 'em all!" As she connected the dots, she got so carried away with her numerical sequences ("Ten! Two! Four!") that she ended up agreeing with herself.

Chandler hated the fact that Kathy's current job called for her to take off her clothes on-stage. Even

Chandler was miraculously cured of his depression after listening to the women discuss which strippers they'd have sex with if they were men. ▼

▲ *The women ended up having a much better time at the strip-club than Chandler.*

Joey finally forgave Chandler for his disloyalty after he spent Thanksgiving crunched up inside a packing crate. That meant that Chandler and Kathy were now free to proclaim their love to the world – or anyway, everyone at Central Perk. But the spectre of Joey still haunted the relationship in **The One with Phoebe's Uterus**. Chandler couldn't bring himself to have "the sex" with Kathy for fear that he would come up short compared to her last boyfriend (Joey). He knew for a fact that Joey was great in bed because they shared a wall. Either that, or Kathy just liked to agree with him a lot. But when Chandler and Kathy finally had "the sex" it was only "fine". Chandler was certain of this, he explained to Monica and Rachel, because Kathy didn't agree with him as strongly as she did with Joey. Monica

worse, she was having simulated onstage sex with a very good-looking guy named Nick. Joey tried to convince Chandler (in **The One with Rachel's Crush**) that people like him and Kathy were actors and that they were there to do a job. The rule, he told him, is that when two actors are actually doing it offstage, the sexual tension between them evaporates. It's when the heat goes away that you gotta get suspicious. Sure enough, the next night when Chandler and Ross went back to the play,

they noticed a distinct lack of intensity between Kathy and her leading man. "Chandler, this is my job," Kathy protested when he accused her of cheating. "I'm playing a part in a play." Turning away, she told him to call her when he grew up. He told him not to expect *that* any time soon. When he went over to Kathy's apartment to apologize later, he found Nick's pants (and Nick).

Demolished by the break-up with Kathy, Chandler stayed in his recliner chair for two days solid in **The One with Joey's Dirty Day**. Joey told the gang not to worry, that this was just Phase 1 of the generic Chandler Depression. It wouldn't be long before he'd get to Phase 2 — which involved porno and massive quantities of alcohol. To cheer him up, the women dragged him out to a strip-club. But while the girls had a great time bonding with the strippers and giving them career advice, Chandler remained catatonic. He insisted on going home and getting back into his chair and his joggers. The girls went with him and tried to get him to open up, but he wasn't ready. Then they started talking about the strippers — and which ones they'd have sex with if they were men. Suddenly Chandler was catapulted into Phase 3. It was a miracle: he was cured. And that meant that it was time for Janice to reappear — which, like a bad penny, she did in **The One with All the Rugby**.

◀ "There's something you've gotta know. If I'm the best, it's only 'cause you made me the best." — Chandler to Monica

MATT
LEBLANC
PROFILE

"Joey is probably the character on *Friends* that has come the longest way over the years," observes director James Burrows, who, after the producers, had the most to do with the shaping of *Friends* during its first season. Joey was originally written as a heartless woman-izer whose caveman sensibility was particularly irksome to a (what was then) more acerbic Monica. But Matt LeBlanc saw Joey as a more complicated person. "I just didn't believe that the women would be friends with this guy who was so crass, self-centred, and hitting on them all the time," he says now. "In having respect for them, he could grow as a character."

"In the pilot Joey was written a lot like Chandler," recalls James Burrows. "But when [the producers] cast Matt, I said,

Matt LeBlanc says that even though he was a model before becoming an actor, he didn't exactly fit the mould – or the clothes. "It was all Dolce and Gabbana and Armani and this one and that one. Their samples are made for stick figures."

"It just seems so futile. All these women and ... nothing. It's like I'm Superman without any powers. I have the cape, and yet I cannot fly."
- Joey in The One With the Lesbian Wedding.

Joey Tribbiani has got one of those old-fashioned Italian families like you only see on TV these days. There are his mother and father who've been married for 25 years. And his Italian-speaking grandmother Noni – whose proudest moment was Joey's stint as Dr. Drake Ramoray on *Days of Our Lives*. He's got seven sisters – all of whom live at home and look almost exactly alike. Oh yeah, there's also Joey's dad's longtime girlfriend – whom his mother knows all about, but pretends not to 'cause it makes him happy – and hey, that's what it's all about, right?

'Just dumb him up a bit.' And they did. Since then, he's gone from a lunkhead to a man who has incredible dimension." Yes, as Joey grew more soulful, he also got dumber – which helped to ameliorate his, well, less high-minded instincts. We know Joey's limitations so well now that he can make a simple "What?" seem funny. The chemistry between him and Chandler gets better and better with each new season. When Joey sets off one of Chandler's slow burns, it's almost as if Laurel and Hardy had come back to life as Nineties urbanites.

Joey Tribbiani may be sweeter than originally envisioned, but he's still not all that enlightened with regard to male–female relationships. Consider him hitting on Rachel while she's still wearing her wedding dress – and dropping his trousers within minutes of meeting Monica. As Lisa Kudrow has observed, "Joey is every girl's nightmare: very sweet, but you know he's eventually going to cheat."

The actor who manages to make all this blatant narcissism funny, and sometimes even endearing, is Matt LeBlanc. He was born in 1967 in the working-class town of Newton, Massachusetts. He is the only child of an Italian-immigrant mother, who raised him in a small apartment while holding down a job as a production supervisor at an electronics company. "It was just me and my mom when I was growing up," says the self-professed Mama's Boy. "We're still very tight." Indeed, the first big-ticket item that Matt bought as his *Friends* money began to kick in was a house for his mom.

"It's the biggest one on the street," he says, "a couple of miles from where I grew up."

As a teenager LeBlanc was considered to be a "gearhead" because he went to a technical vocational high school and majored in carpentry. Although he learnt his craft well enough to earn a living at it, he was mostly interested in partying and messing around with motorcycles and cars. He had his first motorcycle at the age of eight, and was soon competing in various amateur competitions with the hope of becoming a pro-racer. Later his mother forced him to find a less hazardous way to use his talents.

At eighteen Matt left Newton to live with his father in Florida. He then moved to New York – where he convinced two flight attendants to let him share their apartment by telling them that he had a trust fund at his disposal – when, in fact, all he had to his name was a $3,000 stash from selling his truck. Once in the big city, he eventually stumbled into modelling. But at 5ft 11in, he was considered too short to get the really high-paying contracts. "Modelling is all about the clothes anyway," Matt says. "I didn't want to stand still all day having my picture taken just to show off a jacket." In the interim, he managed to make ends meet by working nights at a little place called Fatburger.

> "You know what's great as the show goes on? The rehearsal process, which is what a sitcom is all about. We know each other so well, all six of us, that the choices are made very readily – the performance choices. So it gets up on its feet so fast these days. It's just because we spend so much time together."
> – Matt LeBlanc

Matt got into acting by doing television commercials for Levi's 501 jeans, Coke, Heinz ketchup and Doritos, among others. He also began auditioning for parts in off-Broadway plays – where, as he puts it, he "fell in love with the craft of acting". In 1988 he enrolled in formal acting classes. Within a year he had moved to Los Angeles and landed a starring role in the television series *TV 101*. That short-lived series was followed by two more flops – *Top of the Heap* and *Vinnie & Bobby*. But the fact that he had won starring roles in so many series in such a short time was a clear indication that he was destined for big things. Still, if not for *Friends*, his career might have stumbled along like Joey Tribbiani's.

Although they laugh about it now, the rest of the *Friends* cast was thoroughly intimidated by LeBlanc during the show's early rehearsal period. Something to do with all that black leather and his sultry image on those 501 jeans ads, it would seem. As David Schwimmer recalls, "I thought, 'Oh great, here's this guy I'm going to be working with for maybe five years, and he's fucking Joe Cool stud.'"

So, who is the real Matt LeBlanc? He's a guys' guy who still plays with his cars and motorcycles

In The One with the Football Joey tried to impress a slick-looking Dutch girl named Margha with his knowledge of geography. He knew where Dutch people came from, he told her . . . Pennsylvania.

It's not easy to make Matt LeBlanc look schlumpy, but costume designer Debra McGuire understands that as an unemployed actor who spends the majority of his time at home in front of the tube, Joey isn't particularly into clothes – with the possible exception of the occasional black leather vest or jacket here and there. Joey did wear an Italian designer suit to an audition for the part of a suave, international guy, and a tux to Ross's wedding, but we've mostly seen him in jeans and flannel shirts over T-shirts during the past five years . Maybe, some day, Debra will be able to dress him in these boyish casuals – if he ever gets steady work.

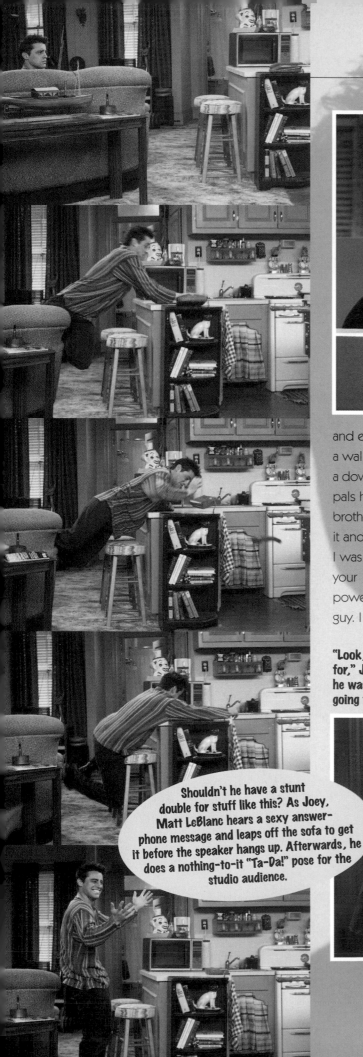

After a hard day of doing nothing, it does a guy good to play Cowboys and Indians. Just ask Joey.

and even races on occasion (despite the fact that he once smashed into a wall trying to cut off Jason Priestley in a celebrity grand prix). He's also a down-to-earth person who's made a concerted effort to hang on to the pals he's had for many years. For the women on the show, he's a kind of brother. "He's the guy who says, 'Hey, they mess with you, tell me about it and I'll take care of them,'" says Jennifer Aniston. "When I first met him I was scared of him, but he's the biggest teddy bear on the planet, like your goombah" And, finally, the big question ... how does his brain power compare with Joey's? Matt LeBlanc puts it best: "I'm not a dumb guy. I just play one on TV."

"Look, I don't know what you're getting so bent out of shape for," Joey told Chandler when he reacted badly to the news that he was moving out of their apartment. "It's not like we were going to live together forever. I mean, we're not Bert and Ernie!"

Shouldn't he have a stunt double for stuff like this? As Joey, Matt LeBlanc hears a sexy answer-phone message and leaps off the sofa to get it before the speaker hangs up. Afterwards, he does a nothing-to-it "Ta-Da!" pose for the studio audience.

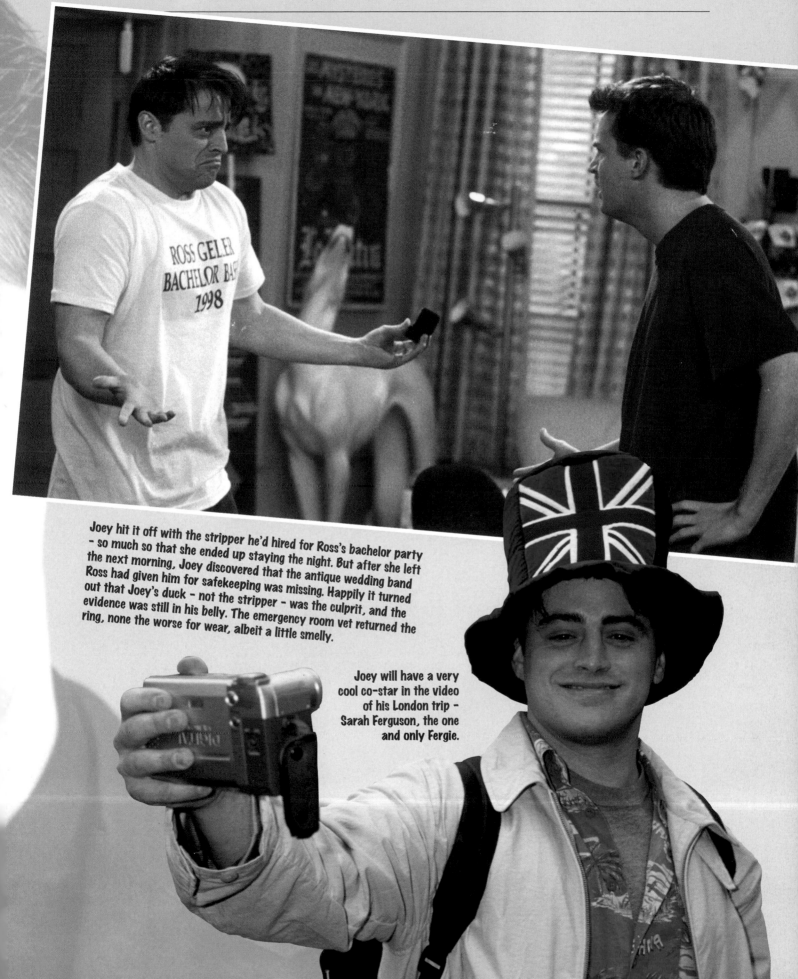

Joey hit it off with the stripper he'd hired for Ross's bachelor party – so much so that she ended up staying the night. But after she left the next morning, Joey discovered that the antique wedding band Ross had given him for safekeeping was missing. Happily it turned out that Joey's duck – not the stripper – was the culprit, and the evidence was still in his belly. The emergency room vet returned the ring, none the worse for wear, albeit a little smelly.

Joey will have a very cool co-star in the video of his London trip – Sarah Ferguson, the one and only Fergie.

THE FOURTH SEASON

We returned from the summer in **The One with the Jellyfish** to find the gang still vacationing on Montauk – where we had left them at the end of the third season. Things weren't pretty then, and they hadn't improved. You might think that discovering her mother would have made Phoebe happy, yet she had nothing but contempt for someone who could abandon her children – no matter how sad the circumstances. Still, when her mother showed up at Central Perk to talk things out a few days later, Phoebe realized to her delight that they had all sorts of things in common; like, for example, they both loved pizza and puppies and The Beatles. There was a bond between them that Phoebe, hurt as she was, could not deny.

Speaking of denial, there was something between Monica, Chandler and Joey that they couldn't deny any longer either. It seemed that when Monica was stung by jellyfish while swimming in the ocean, Chandler had peed on her to neutralize the sting.

▲ Phoebe bonds with her dead mother in the guise of a cat named Julio.

"And the winnah is..." A British Academy of Film and Television Arts Award went to Friends in 1997.

It's all got to be perfect – even a white chef's jacket. Friends costume designer Debra McGuire tweaks Courteney Cox's chef costume wear on the set.

Rachel is so, so happy that Ross is man enough to admit that their break-up was all his fault.

Joey trips the light fantastic with the building super, Mr Treeger, in The One with the Ballroom Dancing. ▼

In **The One with the Cat** Phoebe, guilty perhaps about all the time she'd been spending with her birth-mother, decided that a cat that had wondered into Central Perk and taken refuge in her guitar case contained the spirit of her dead adopted mother, Lily. Ross, who thought this was pathetic New Age hokum, eventually had to apologize to Phoebe's mother (the cat), after Phoebe shamed him by explaining how much it meant to her to have her dead mother back. But being an animal freak, she nevertheless felt obligated to return her mother to her other life – in which she was a male cat named Julio.

In **The One with the Ballroom Dancing)** Joey almost got Monica evicted (for illegally subletting her grandmother's apartment). Fortunately, the snippy super, Mr Treeger, needed something from Joey – help with his ballroom-dancing technique. It seemed that he wanted to make a good impression on a lady at the Super Ball.

The magic makers – guest star Penn Jillette and former David Copperfield producer Kevin S. Bright – talk some shop on the Friends set.

Happily, Joey made a great dance partner – and he and Treeger found something really special during their time together. Before he went off to try his luck with a real girl, Treeger and Joey did a Fred and Ginger against the glamorous backdrop of the Manhattan skyline.

Romantic frustration swirled around everyone (even Gunther) in both **The One with Joey's New Girlfriend** and **The One with the Dirty Girl**. The first victim was Chandler – who developed a terrible crush on a girl Joey was dating. Her name was Kathy, and she and Joey had met in acting class. He revealed his feelings to Joey, but his confession was so hysterical that Joey thought he was (over) acting.

Next it was Ross's turn to lose it, when what he thought was going to be a romantic night at home with Amanda, the lovely mother of one of Ben's little friends, metamorphosed into his babysitting the kids while she went out. This humiliation didn't help Ross in the undeclared competition he was having with Rachel over who would be the first to find someone new. But it's not as if things were so much better for Rachel. Her boyfriend of the moment was a really young guy, Josh, who acted even younger (and goofier) than he looked. And not only that … he was stealing from her. At least Ross had made ten bucks on his relationship, he told her happily.

"OK, I have a really enormous crush on you," Phoebe tells Rick.
"But because you're a client I can't ask you out, even though you give me, you know, the Feelings." ▼

It was England's famed Channel Four that first proposed the idea of a *Friends* London excursion to the show's producers during the summer hiatus of 1997. Much as they loved the idea, Marta Kauffman and David Crane already had big things planned for their characters in the coming season. To add a plot turn this complicated and, admittedly, this improbable was going to require shaking things up in a seismic fashion. And that meant zeroing in on two major unresolved issues that had been hotly debated between them and the writers since the show's inception. "We had to come up with a storyline that would cause all the Friends to go to London," says producer/writer Greg Malins. "And that ended up being Ross getting married, because they would all have to go to his wedding." The only hitch was how to get from "Ross meets someone" to "Ross is going to England to get married" in six episodes.

Surprise … it turns out that Lisa Kudrow doesn't dress in flowery Phoebe-wear off camera. She sticks to tailored separates with classic lines. That's what she told In Style magazine, anyway.

Over at Central Perk, Phoebe, who had got herself fired by getting too friendly with one of her massage clients, was forced to keep singing even though she had a terrible cold. But to her delight the cold gave her a sexily husky singing voice – and a whole new world-weary, chanteuse-y persona. She was dismayed when her health and her real voice returned – so much so that she tried, unsuccessfully, to re-catch the cold from the many people she had infected.

Does Ross ever work? Not in **The One with the Dirty Girl** – where he appeared to be spending all his

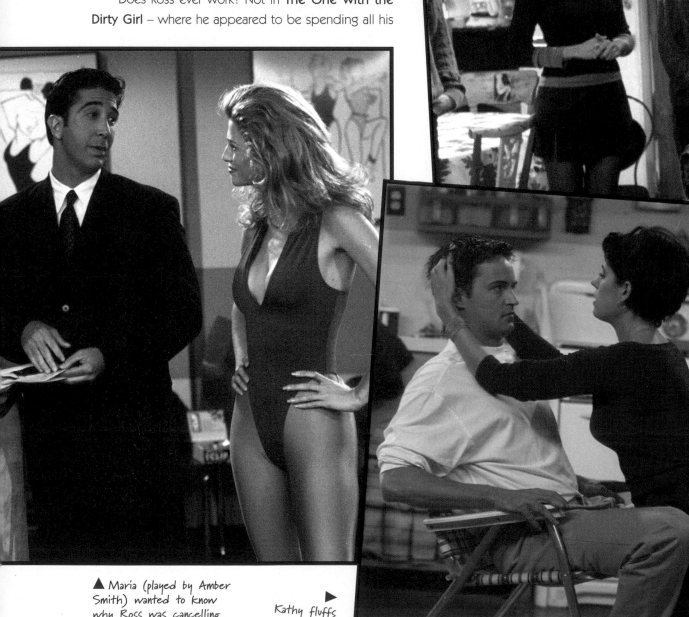

▲ Maria (played by Amber Smith) wanted to know why Ross was cancelling his gym membership.

► Kathy fluffs Chandler's hair ...

◄ Joey lets Chandler off the hook — and out of the box.

Seeing his chance, Chandler urged him to make a choice between the two women, lobbying way too enthusiastically on behalf of Casey. Joey decided to go with Kathy, so Chandler had no choice but to tell him the truth. And he was about to do just that when Joey told him that Kathy had just broken up with him – maybe, he was thinking, because she was into another guy. The words came tumbling out of Chandler's mouth: he was Kathy's Other Guy, he admitted. And not only that. He had kissed her. Joey was beyond pissed – not so much from the idea of losing Kathy, but rather that his best friend had gone behind his back.

Joey was so furious (in **The One with Chandler in a Box**) that he decided he didn't want to live with someone who didn't know how to be a friend. "If we still had that entertainment unit, I'd get in there for six hours," Chandler pleaded, "and think about how I'd let you down." Suddenly Joey was interested. "We got a box," he said brightly. And that's how Chandler came to spend Thanksgiving night in a crate – while the others gathered for Monica's annual feast. Then Kathy showed up unannounced to apologize to Joey and bid Chandler adieu. Addressing an airhole in the box, she told him that she couldn't bear to come between two best friends. It was better, she thought, if they didn't see each other again. Chandler, who had promised Joey not to say another word, said nothing –

time trying to find Ms Right. Cheryl, the incredibly beautiful girl he went out with next, turned out to be a secret slob. Her place was piled high with garbage and leftover food. At one point Ross lashed out at a furry thing that scurried under a pile of papers. Alarmed by the commotion, Cheryl came running out of her bedroom. She was afraid he'd killed her hamster, but, happily, it was only a rat.

By **The One Where Chandler Crosses the Line**, Chandler's crush on Kathy (Joey's girlfriend) had become unbearable – after he accidentally saw her getting out of the shower naked. But stunning as Kathy was, it didn't stop Joey from getting interested in a new girl named Casey.

> "If an actor is saying, 'I don't know how to make this line work,' you can sit there all day long and tell them why it works, but if they don't feel it, they're not going to be able to make it work. So it's incumbent upon you to change it so that it *is* comfortable for them. One thing that has never been said to any actor on the *Friends* stage is, 'Just do the line as it's written. It's fine.'"
> – Kevin S. Bright

but instead poked his finger out of the little hole to wiggle his sad good-bye.

Monica landed her dream job (in **The One with the Girl from Poughkeepsie**), but the workers at the restaurant tried to get her to leave by all sorts of nasty little tricks – like writing "Quit Bitch" on her chef's toque. To show them she was not to be messed with, she cooked up a plan with Joey wherein she would hire him as a waiter and then fire him in front of the employees after he razzed her. But when

Joey found out how good the tips were at the restaurant, he changed his mind. He proposed a new plan: he would gain everyone's trust, then they would be more open to all the nice things he was going to say about her. But after getting locked in the deep-freeze and falling into a vat of marinara sauce, Monica lost it big time. "I'm a good person," she sobbed, "and I don't deserve this." Feeling terrible for her, Joey returned to the original script; he dissed her and she told him to take a walk.

Phoebe's half-brother, Frank Jr, had come up with an interesting idea that would keep her busy in **The One with Phoebe's Uterus**: he and Alice had got married, and they wanted her to have their baby. (Because they couldn't, obviously.) She decided to go for it, but the gang wasn't exactly enthusiastic and their negativity about Frank Jr's proposal hurt Phoebe. They'd been a lot more supportive, she pointed out, when she'd decided to make denim furniture.

Phoebe was under a lot of strain in **The One with the Embryos**. For one thing, there was only a 25 per cent chance that one of the implanted embryos would survive. Not only that, it cost $16,000 for each try – and that was all the money Frank Jr and Alice had in the world. But Phoebe

▲ Joey wanted to come through for Monica. Really. It's just that it had been a long time since he had had the kind of cash in his pocket that he'd earned while waiting tables in her restaurant.

David Schwimmer gets serious with Total TV magazine.

"There is this thing that we talk about sometimes, especially on *Friends* – a laugh that you're not proud of – where, yeah, they laughed, but all you had to do was say the word 'nipple' and they'd laugh. Or 'lesbian'. For some reason, just throw that word in, they laugh big. So it's not always enough (just to get a laugh). Especially when you're trying to do more." – Marta Kauffman

had a sincere heart-to-heart with the embryos, asking them to really "hang on" to her uterus and not to get upset if she was screaming the next time they saw her. As she waited for the results from a home pregnancy test, she occupied herself by singing a song called "Are You In There, Little Foetus?" Happily, as she soon discovered, they were.

Meanwhile, Monica and Rachel got caught up in a heated battle with Chandler and Joey over which pair of roommates knew the other better. The dispute was to be settled with a game (invented by Ross) using little-known

Phoebe's mother brought her a puppy and told her she would return to pick it up in three days. She hoped this would make Phoebe understand how painful it is to give up a baby – even if it's not your own. ▼

secrets about the Friends. The categories were Fears and Pet Peeves, Literature, and It's All Relative. The stakes were high: the duck and the chick versus Monica's apartment. The contest was fairly even until the Lightning Round when Ross asked Monica and Rachel what Chandler did for a living. They stammered, they stuttered, and they faked it as best they could, but the truth was they had no idea. The next thing we saw was Joey and Chandler moving their foose-ball table into their fabulous new apartment across the hall.

In **The One with Rachel's Crush** Bloomingdale's reassigned Rachel as a

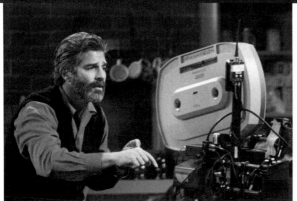

Director Michael Lembeck won an Emmy for The One with the Superbowl, Parts I & II.

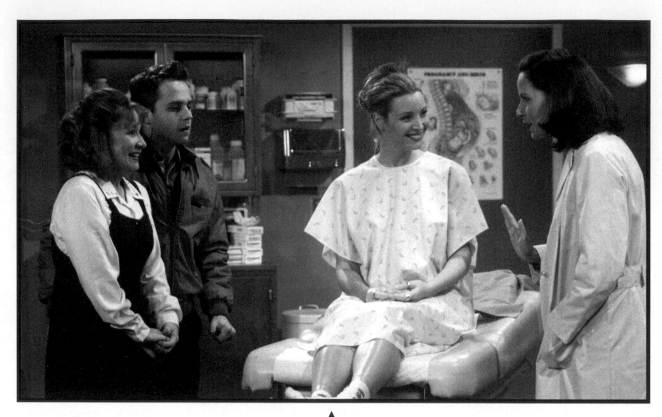

▲

There was plenty of pressure on Phoebe and her uterus to get it right the first time with the implantation of the embryos because it cost $16,000 a pop — and that was all the money that Frank Jr and Alice had in the world.

"personal shopper". Her first client turned out to be a very cute guy named Joshua. She tried and tried to get him interested in her, and her efforts finally paid off when he invited her to a club opening (in **The One with Joey's Dirty Day**). There was only one little problem: she had already promised her boss that she would entertain his niece Emily, who was visiting New York from England. Ross allowed Rachel to bulldoze him into taking over her hosting duties, and he was glad he had once he got to know the lovely Emily.

In The One with All the Rugby, Ross did his best to be as macho as Emily's big bruiser British friends, by getting into a fierce game of rugby (whatever *that* was) with them. Not surprisingly, he got badly banged up. Emily was really frightened for him — and really touched.

With Ross being all starry-eyed over Emily, Rachel was more determined than ever to get something going with Joshua (in **The One with the Fake Party**). However, her technique was decidedly weird. Like, she got him to come over for a "going-away party" for Emily, then in a deluded attempt to be sexy, told him seductively that she could tie a knot in a cherry stem with her

Charlton Heston (with Kevin S. Bright, David Crane and Marta Kauffman on the set of The One with Joey's Dirty Day) claims that he had no idea who the Friends on *Friends* were until he made a recent guest appearance on the show. "When my agent called, I said, 'What is *Friends*? Whose friends?' He said, 'It's a TV show.'" Heston was very pleased with his little guest-starring stint on whadaya-callit. "I really enjoyed doing it," he says fondly. "They paid me an obscene amount of money."

tongue. She then proceeded to have a choking fit trying to do it.

Finally, in exasperation, Rachel just went with the truth: this whole manic routine was her way of trying to seduce him, she said. Actually, he confessed, he liked her, too – even if she was a little nuts. However, Joshua had a big But. The thing was that he had just got divorced, and he needed a little time before he got involved with someone again. Oh well, the party wasn't a total loss for Rachel; at least she had ruined Ross's last night with Emily.

With Emily back in England, Ross realized that he not only missed her, but he had fallen in love with her. And Emily was in love with Ross too. She headed right back for New York.

While getting an ultrasound, Phoebe discovered that she was carrying triplets. Frank Jr and Alice were overjoyed … at first. And then they realized the financial implications of their imminent instant family. Phoebe was worried for them, too. So, to earn extra money, she decided to combine her skills as a masseuse with the old van she'd bought for the catering business to create

Joey and Chandler get into the spirit of things as Rachel decides to throw an impromptu (and unwelcome) going-away party for Emily in The One with the Fake Party.

In her January 1998 interview with *Jane* magazine, Courteney Cox said, "On a perfect day, my call time would be at 11, so I can sleep in. When I get to work, Craft Services has my favourite breakfast: egg whites, turkey, bacon and tomatoes. There are flowers in my dressing room from a wonderful person who couldn't make me happier. The note says, 'I just wanted to tell you I love you. No strings attached. I'm committed to you, you're not committed to me, and that's OK. You don't even have to call.'"

"I saw things in terms of black and white, right and wrong," Lisa Kudrow told Parade magazine in May 1998. "I felt all actors were idiots whose lives didn't work. If I became one, I thought people wouldn't take me seriously."

PHOEBE'S SONGS

Smelly Cat

Chorus:
Smelly Cat, smelly cat what are they feeding you?
Smelly Cat, smelly cat it's not your fault ...

They won't take you to the vet.
You're obviously not their favourite pet.
You may not be a bed of roses,
And you're no friend to those with noses.

Smelly cat, smelly cat what are they feeding you?
Smelly cat, smelly cat it's not your fault!

Two of Them Kissed (Last Night)

There was a girl. We'll call her Betty.
And a guy. Let's call him Neil.
Now, I can't stress this point too strongly,
This story isn't real.

(...)

Now our Neil must decide,
Who will be the girl that he casts aside.
Will Betty be the one who he loves truly,
Or will it be the one who we'll call ...Lulie

He MUST decide, he MUST decide,
Even though I made him up he MUST decide ...

Don't

They'll be times when you get older
When you'll want to sleep with people
Just to make them like you ...
But don't.

Chorus:
Cause that's another thing that you don't wanna do. Everbody!
That's another thing that you don't wanna do.

Terry's a Jerk

Terry's a jerk!
And he won't let me work!
And I hate Central Perk!
(...)
And you're all invited to bite me!

The Book of Lore

Sometimes men love women,
Sometimes men love men,
And then there are bisexuals,
Though some just say they're kidding themselves
La la-la-la la-la-la-la-la-la-la ...

The Snowman

I made a man with eyes of coal
And a smile so bewitchin'.
How was I supposed to know
That my mom was dead in the kitchen?
La la-la-la la-la-la-la-la-la-la...

The Animal Song

Oh, the cow in the meadow goes moo,
Oh, the cow in the meadow goes moo.
Then the farmer hits him on the head and
grinds him up,
And that's how we get hamburgers!

Nooowww, chickens!

Mother's Ashes

My mother's ashes,
Even her eyelashes,
Are resting in a little, yellow jar.

And sometimes when it's breezy,
Or if I'm feeling sneezy,
And now I ...

Excuse me! Excuse me!
Yeah, noisy boys!

BLACKOUT

NEW YORK CITY HAS NO POWER.
AND THE MILK IS GETTING SOUR.
BUT TO ME THIS IS NOT SCARY,
'CAUSE I STAY AWAY FROM DAIRY.

Phoebe

Love Song ♡

You don't have to be awake to be my
men
Long as you have brainwaves,
I'll be there to hold your hand.
Tho' we just met the other day
There's something I have got to say ...
Thank you, that's all.

Shower Song

I'm in the shower and I'm writing a song,
Stop me if you've heard it,
My skin is soapy and my hair is wet,
And Tegrin spelled backwards is Nirget.

Chorus:
Lather, rinse, repeat,
And lather, rinse, repeat,
And lather, rinse, repeat,
As needed.

a totally new enterprise called 'Relaxi-Taxi'. This was zany even for Phoebe. But then, she had been doing all sorts of weird things lately – like eating meat and having her morning sickness in the evening.

Rachel was doing some odd (read: desperate) things too in **The One with Rachel's New Dress**. She had Monica whip up a fabulous dinner (which she would take credit for), and then she picked out a dress to seduce Joshua in. Well, not a dress exactly. More like a kind of lacy under-thing. The two of them ended up in his parents' apartment – where Joshua was staying while they were travelling in Europe. Naturally they came home early and caught her in (what there was of) her lacy seduction get-up.

No doubt about it, things just weren't going Rachel's way. Not only was Ross getting married, but she was stuck in Joey and Chandler's apartment while they were living it up across the hall. So (in **The One with All the Haste**) Rachel and Monica cooked up a plan to get the guys to trade apartments in exchange for centre-court season tickets for the Knicks. Joey was totally down for the swap and, besides, he told Chandler, the timing was perfect because he'd just clogged the toilet. While the guys were out at the basketball game that night, Rachel and Monica switched all the furniture back into their respective apartments. They knew the guys were going to go crazy, and they did, but then they made them an offer they couldn't refuse; in order to keep their apartment, Monica and Rachel would kiss each other (on the lips) for one full minute. "That was one goooood minute," Joey said happily.

All too soon it was time for Emily to head home to England again. Ross was going to miss not only Emily, he realized, but also the person he became when he was with her – right down to the new earring she'd talked him into getting. (Chandler thought it made him look like he was in Wham.) He tried to get her to stay – even if only for a day, but she was afraid of losing her job. While talking to Chandler and Joey at the coffee house, Ross realized that he wanted Emily to move in with him. The idea didn't quite make sense to her ... after all, it

> "When we first got a Japanese-dubbed version of *Friends*, we were amused by the attempt to get the characterization of the voices right. In the Japanese version, Phoebe was really high-pitched, really amped up. And Ross's character was kind of down and, you know, duhhh."
> – Kevin S. Bright

wasn't like they were getting married or anything. Then they would get married, Ross said quickly; and he got down on one knee, pulled out his new earring (ouch!) and placed it (halfway) on Emily's finger.

In **The One with All the Wedding Dresses**, Ross had the nerve to ask Rachel how she "was" about his getting married. That did it. Now Rachel was going to have to marry Joshua. Wasting no time, she popped the question to Joshua the following day. Stammering, Joshua told her, "No", but "Thanks!". And with that, he was gone.

Of course, weddings were always on Monica's mind – but never more so than after she picked up Emily's gown from the bridal shop. Passing herself off as Emily, she had tried it on in the store, and couldn't resist

putting it on again when she got home. And then Phoebe put in a surprise appearance wearing a maternity wedding gown that she had rented from the Last Chance Bridal Shop.

Donning her old wedding dress, Rachel joined the girly fun and the three faux brides drank beer and ate popcorn and had a smashing good time. Then the doorbell rang and, thinking it was Chandler, Rachel (still dressed in her bridal drag) threw open the door and shouted, "I do!" as a little joke. But it wasn't Chandler at the door, it was Joshua.

In **The One with the Invitation** Ross began to make out Rachel's invitation – until Emily said that she didn't think *she'd* be

▲ Courteney Cox and Matthew Perry kick back and relax during a rehearsal break.

◄ Frank Jr and his wife Alice were overjoyed at the news that Phoebe was pregnant with not one, but three, babies. But it didn't take long for the reality of the situation to set in.

That was one goooood kiss. Joey will always look back fondly on Rachel and Monica's long, passionate kiss.

comfortable with having any of *her* old lovers there. As he debated what to do, a cascade of Rachel memories flowed through his mind. How could he not invite her after all they'd been through together?

After Rachel received her invitation, she, too, was forced to confront her true feelings for Ross and his marriage to Emily. She wasn't entirely sure why, but there was no way she could bring herself to go to London for the wedding.

But Rachel had plenty to keep her mind occupied (in **The One with the Worst Best Man Ever**) with looking after Phoebe who was having terrible mood swings – laughing one second, crying the next. While overhearing the guys talking about Ross's bachelor party, it occurred to her and Monica that a baby shower might be just the thing to cheer Phoebe up. But that backfired when everyone gave Phoebe presents for her instead of the babies – the reasoning being that she was only going to have to give them up anyway.

▶

Phoebe apologized to Monica and Rachel for being so irritable at the baby shower they had thrown her. She pinned the blame on the terrible mood swings she'd been having lately — along with the realization that she couldn't keep all those adorable baby presents ... not to mention the babies themselves.

Phoebe rented a maternity wedding gown at the Last Chance Bridal Shop, so she could play Catch the Corsage with Monica. ▼

Things got really awkward when the time came for Ross to pick his best man. Both Joey and Chandler were expecting to be chosen, but Ross had already picked Chandler – and it was pretty clear to Joey that he'd never even been in the running. Joey was crushed until Chandler said he could be *his* best man. That hurt Ross, who had always assumed that that honour would go to him. Finally Chandler threw up his hands and said he wasn't going to get married anyway, so what was the big deal? If that's how it was, Ross said, then Joey would be his best man. And to mark the occasion, he gave Emily's wedding ring to him for safekeeping.

Proud of his newly upgraded status, Joey got right into the swing of things by having a stripper for Ross's bachelor party. The entertainment was a hit with all the invited guests – including Chandler, Joey, Gunther and a few of Ross's fellow museum geeks. As the stripper was packing up to leave, she hinted to Joey that she might like to hang around with him after everyone went home. But after she'd gone the next morning, Joey discovered that the ring Ross had entrusted to him was gone, too. The guys decided to set up a sting for the

▲ Ross: "Hey, what are those?" Joey: "Little party favours. Check it out!"

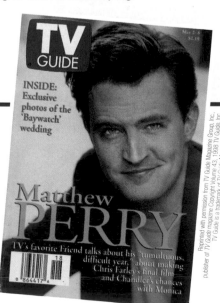

2 May 1998
Could he be any more interesting? Matthew Perry talks openly and hilariously to TV Guide about his life away from Friends.

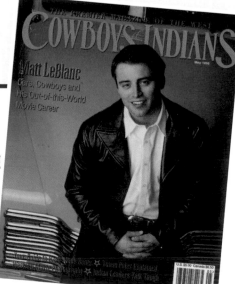

"All my friends call me a gearhead – ask anyone who knows me," Matt LeBlanc told Cowboys & Indians magazine in May 1998. "I replace my own roller rockers on my Suburban. And I do my own oil changes on all my cars – and that includes the Pantera race car and the Jeep Cherokee."

▲ He was a little nervous about remembering his lines, but Richard Branson pulled off his Friends cameo like a pro. Here he gets to know his co-stars while waiting for the next camera set-up.

stripper, booking her for a quickie at Chandler's office, where all three of them would then confront her with her crime. But the stripper made a very convincing case for herself. She earned 1,600 dollars a week, she told them huffily. What did she need with a stupid ring? Eventually they discovered that Joey's duck was the culprit and the evidence was still in his belly. The Emergency Room vet returned the ring, none the worse for wear, although a little smelly.

Joey was just so mortified by the whole duck-swallowing-the-wedding-ring nightmare that he insisted Chandler take over as best man. But Ross, touched by both friends' concern, knew what he had to do; he wanted them *both* to be his best man. That made all three of them tear up, although they would rather have sung "Feelings" in a karaoke bar than let the others see.

There were two major unresolved issues that had been hotly debated between Marta Kauffman, David Crane and the writers since the show's inception. As writer/producer Michael Borkow explains: "Did we want Ross to actually get married? And did we want Monica and Chandler to sleep together? There were strong - really strong - feelings both for and against."

Rumour: the Queen banned the Friends crew from filming a sequence in front of Buckingham Palace because she was unhappy with some unflattering remarks made by Fergie when she appeared on the Oprah Winfrey Show.

Courtesy of Hello Magazine

Fact: the Palace administration only allows the Queen's London residence to be filmed for documentaries and news items. An official spokesperson stressed that there could be no exceptions, even for the monarch's former daughter-in-law.

In **The One with Ross's Wedding, Parts I & II**, everyone was off to London for the time of their lives. Make that everyone except Phoebe – who couldn't fly during her last trimester – and Rachel. Phoebe understood Rachel's misgivings just fine. "If someone I was still in love with was getting married," she began, but Rachel stopped her right there. What? She was *not* in love with Ross, she sputtered, but her words got all tangled up and she said just the opposite … that she *was* in love with Ross and she *did* have sexual feelings for him. Phoebe tried some aversion therapy – which consisted of bopping Rachel on the head whenever she thought about Ross. But nothing was going to make Rachel stop loving Ross. Not even the fact that he was getting married. And so, she reasoned, it was only fair that she fly to London and tell Ross how she felt – so he could make an informed decision.

Meanwhile, all was not well in England. Demolition had begun early on the hallowed old hall that Emily had set her heart on, so they didn't even have a place for the ceremony. The food and the flowers were coming out all wrong. And battles were breaking out between everyone from the bride and groom's parents to Joey and Chandler. Monica's mother kept making little gibes about how she would never get married. And then, at the rehearsal dinner, one of the guests thought Monica was Ross's mother. Joey was missing America – even though he got to hang out with a certain duchess named Fergie. And last, but certainly not least: Chandler and Monica spent the night together. (Although no one found out, thank goodness.)

Into the middle of all this chaos walked Rachel – despite Phoebe's best efforts to get

"I heard Joan Collins' voice in my head when I was working on my character Andrea Waltham," says Jennifer Saunders, "and that's a frightening thing to have happen, I can tell you."

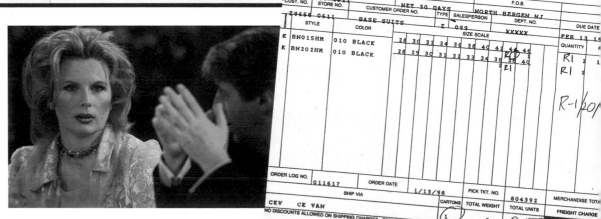

◄ Does anyone have any reason why these two should not be married? Emily will in a matter of moments.

the gang to head her off before she got to Ross. But she happened to make her entrance as Ross and Emily were having a tender pre-wedding huddle. Seeing them together, Rachel couldn't bring herself to interfere. So, instead of telling Ross that she loved him, she told him only that she wished him congratulations.

The whole wedding production was more than a little unorthodox. For one thing, the hall looked as if it had been bombed. In addition, there were two best men, and one of them (Joey) was talking on a mobile phone as he made his way up the aisle. (It was Phoebe in New York, still frantic that Rachel was going to ruin the wedding.)

Next down the aisle were Chandler and Monica. "What we did last night was stupid," Chandler whispered. "What were we thinking?" she hissed back. "I'm coming over tonight though, right?" he asked. "Oh yeah, definitely," Monica answered.

But crazy as the whole scene was, it was nothing compared to what came next. After the registrar read the wedding vows, the bride and groom dutifully repeated them. "I, Ross," Ross said, "take thee, *Rachel* ..." Realizing what had come out of his mouth, he quickly corrected himself, "take thee, *Emily*." As the wedding guests watched in stunned silence, theregistrar stammered, "Shall I go on?"

Nothing but the best will do. Chandler and Joey wore Calvin for Ross's wedding.

A phalanx of fans and photographers cheered on Matthew Perry and Matt LeBlanc as they filmed their break-up scene in front of Westminster Abbey.

MATTHEW PERRY PROFILE

Could he have *had* a better year? The answer is uh-uh, no way. Together with his partner in comedy Courteney Cox, Matthew Perry has played a major part in making *Friends'* fifth season its best ever. It's not just that he spins his quips like nobody else (although he does), but that he's been able to imbue Chandler with so many new colours. "For the first three years, I was just kinda saying the funny lines," he observes. "Now I can play some emotional stuff."

> **"I was on every cancelled show that George Clooney wasn't on." – Matthew Perry**

There but for the grace of Chandler's many neuroses would have gone Joey. That's right: Monica was tentatively charted to hook up with Joey in the show's original master plan. (You can see her wowed reaction to her hunky new neighbour – a silently mouthed "oh my god" – in **The One with the Flashback**.) But, ultimately, the producers decided that the obsessive Monica and the tormented Chandler would make for a more volatile duo – and a funnier one, too. Matthew Perry was all for it: "Those two characters, I think, are the most neurotic of all the Friends," he says. "So seeing two really neurotic people trying to have a relationship with each other – with lots of ups and downs and probably break-ups and then getting back together – makes for a very high-energy kind of pace."

TV viewers sometimes assume that their series favourites just make up their lines as they go along. But Matthew Perry is the one case where the exception is often the rule. The more time the writers spent with Matthew, the more his idiosyncratic speech cadences began to crop up in Chandler's dialogue. Before long, Matthew's own real-life misadventures had seeped into the show's plot twists, too. After listening to him describe a date from hell along with his fears of ending up alone, for example, the writers wove the incident into a Chandler story arc. "I'm not dead," Chandler would moan after a disastrous romantic encounter, "and yet I have no life." Over the past few seasons, many of Matthew's suggestions for jokes

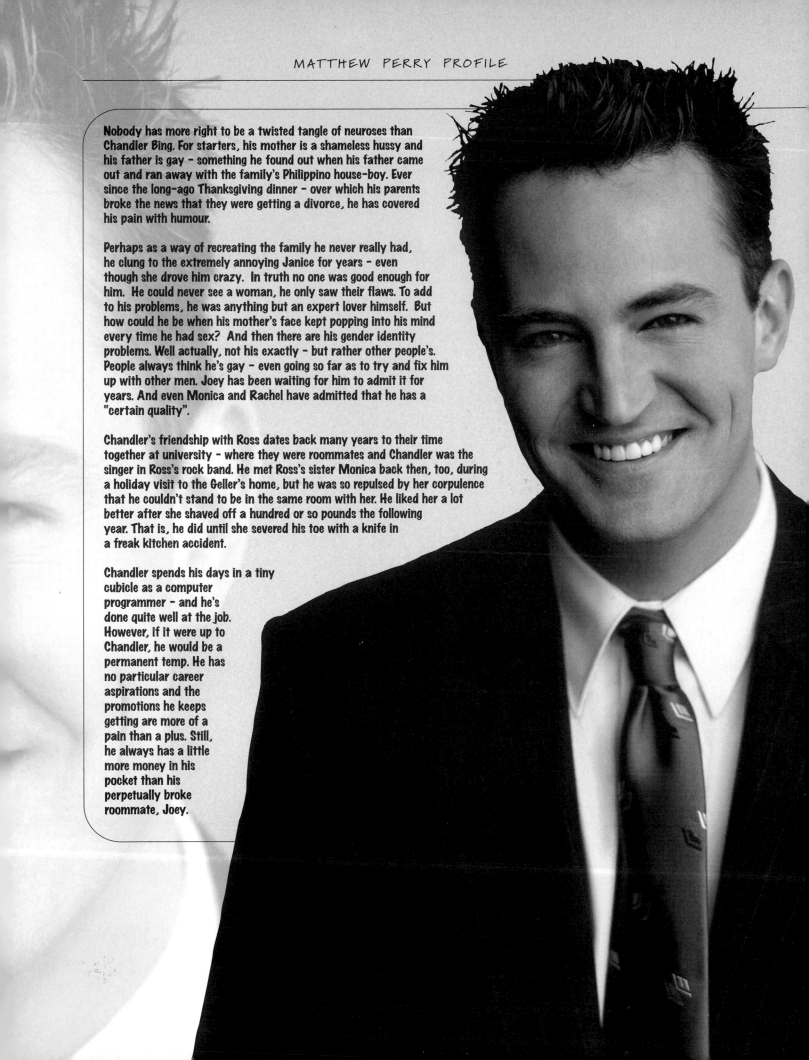

Nobody has more right to be a twisted tangle of neuroses than Chandler Bing. For starters, his mother is a shameless hussy and his father is gay – something he found out when his father came out and ran away with the family's Philippino house-boy. Ever since the long-ago Thanksgiving dinner – over which his parents broke the news that they were getting a divorce, he has covered his pain with humour.

Perhaps as a way of recreating the family he never really had, he clung to the extremely annoying Janice for years – even though she drove him crazy. In truth no one was good enough for him. He could never see a woman, he only saw their flaws. To add to his problems, he was anything but an expert lover himself. But how could he be when his mother's face kept popping into his mind every time he had sex? And then there are his gender identity problems. Well actually, not his exactly – but rather other people's. People always think he's gay – even going so far as to try and fix him up with other men. Joey has been waiting for him to admit it for years. And even Monica and Rachel have admitted that he has a "certain quality".

Chandler's friendship with Ross dates back many years to their time together at university – where they were roommates and Chandler was the singer in Ross's rock band. He met Ross's sister Monica back then, too, during a holiday visit to the Geller's home, but he was so repulsed by her corpulence that he couldn't stand to be in the same room with her. He liked her a lot better after she shaved off a hundred or so pounds the following year. That is, he did until she severed his toe with a knife in a freak kitchen accident.

Chandler spends his days in a tiny cubicle as a computer programmer – and he's done quite well at the job. However, if it were up to Chandler, he would be a permanent temp. He has no particular career aspirations and the promotions he keeps getting are more of a pain than a plus. Still, he always has a little more money in his pocket than his perpetually broke roommate, Joey.

Chandler and Joey. Matthew and Matt.
All four of these guys are really buds.

and plot turns have found their way into the show, and he is the only Friend who has spent working time in the writers' room.

All this creative give-and-take is a welcome change for Matthew, who thinks of himself as a writer as much as an actor. On his earlier sitcom outings, he had felt stifled creatively. "I was convinced I could write something better than the things I had been in on television," he says of the period in the early 1990s when he began writing scripts. Not only had he co-written a sitcom pilot that had caught the eye of the NBC brass, he co-wrote a movie called *Imagining Emily* about a man who falls in love with a grown-up version of his imaginary childhood friend. By the way, his sitcom was called *Maxwell House* and it was about a group of friends who sat around a New York coffee house talking about their lives. By all accounts, the script was pretty sharp. The problem was that NBC already had something remarkably like it in the works.

Born in 1969, in Williamstown, Massachusetts, he is the son of actor John Perry – familiar in the 1960s as the face of the Old Spice cologne – and Suzanne Perry, then a model. Like

Chandler backs Joey up with a full bottle of washing liquid as they prepare to meet Joey's stalker.

He's not exactly a clothes-horse, but Chandler Bing does have his own distinctive sartorial style. The others make fun of him for his prissy sweater vests, and it's true he does have quite a large collection. But he also shows up in hip seventies-style sports shirts quite often. Suits (with a tie and a sweater vest) are his uniform at the office, and he wears sweats and a T-shirt when he's depressed or vegging-out in his recliner.

Could he *be* any more white trash? Chandler and Joey were left with only a canoe, a lawn chair and a duck after a sly burglar talked Joey into locking himself in his entertainment unit while he cleaned the place out.

Chandler let Joey into his hotel bedroom only because Joey knew that the "hot girl" in there with him was Monica.

Chandler's, his parents' marriage was cut short by divorce. Before his first birthday he and his mother moved to her native Ottawa, the city he still considers home. His mother began working in several different capacities within Canada's federal Liberal party. She and young Matthew moved around a lot during this period, but ultimately they settled again in Ottawa in 1978 when she became a press aide to Pierre Trudeau. "My recollection of that time mostly was, 'Wow, she's working a lot, and I wish she wasn't,'" he recalls. As for school, Perry says, "I was a horrible student." He spent much of the day at Ottawa's exclusive Ashbury College just goofing around – and honing the unusual verbal tic he shares with Chandler – a way of emphasizing certain words for satirical effect. However, his mother remembers him as being more determined than comical as a child. "He's very, very, very serious," she says. From an early age her son had a clear set of priorities – and school was not among them. "He used to say to me, 'Why do I have to go to school? I will never use this. I want to play tennis and I want to act.'"

Matthew spent his childhood on the tennis court. "When everybody else was hanging out, I was going down to the tennis club, which was frequented primarily by 60-year-old men, and hoping that one of them wouldn't show up, so I could be the fourth in a doubles match." By the time he was thirteen, he was the No. 2 player in Ottawa. In doubles, he and his partner achieved third at the Canadian National Championships in his age group. Because his goal was to play professional tennis, he decided to head for Los

Angeles to live with his father, who had moved there to act. "It was an opportunity for me to get to know him," he says. His mother moved to L.A. herself two years later. Matthew continued to compete in tournaments until he lost a big match in front of his whole family. It didn't help that he had begun to vent his frustration on the court in the manner of his idol, Jimmy Connors. "Nine times out of ten, I'd win, but I'd still be upset," he recalls. "So I completely stopped playing after graduation."

His tennis dreams were quickly abandoned after he was "discovered" by director William Richert at the age of fifteen. He was playing hooky from class and sitting in a restaurant with three girls. "I was trying to be funny in an effort to impress them – and I got a note on a napkin from Richert saying he would really like me to be in his next movie, and to call him. So I did, and two months later I was on the set of *A Night in the Life of Jimmy Reardon* in Chicago [opposite River Phoenix]. This would be a much better story if the movie had been a huge success."

Matthew starred in four failed series and did dozens of guest-star roles, as well as another film (*She's Out of Control*), before landing *Friends*. More recently he has starred in *Fools Rush In* and *Edwards and Hunt* with the late Chris Farley. Although notoriously insecure and tough on himself, he acknowledges that whatever happens in his big-screen career, he has a great day job to fall back on. He might even know now that the thing his millions of fans love most about Chandler Bing is watching Matthew Perry play himself.

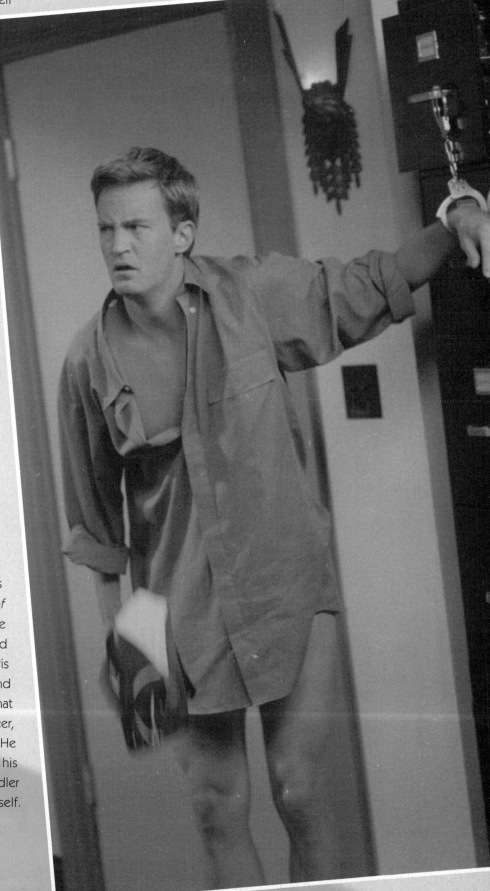

It looks like Chandler's sex-play with Rachel's boss Joanna got a little out-of-hand.

THE BALLAD OF ROSS AND RACHEL

At first glance, it might appear that **Ross Geller**'s entire romantic history is completely caught up in his on-again-off-again involvement with Rachel Green. But for someone who gets so flustered and shy around the opposite sex, Ross has done pretty well with women over the years.

Celia, the Bug Lady from the museum was a babe and she really liked Ross; in fact, she liked him so much she wanted him to talk dirty to her while they were making (or trying to make) love. But that kind of foreplay just wasn't Ross's thing. Not that he didn't try. Still, after

▲ The calm before the storm: Ross and Rachel snuggle before she discovers The List.

◄ Ross thought his newborn baby son, Ben, looked like his Uncle Ed covered in Jell-O.

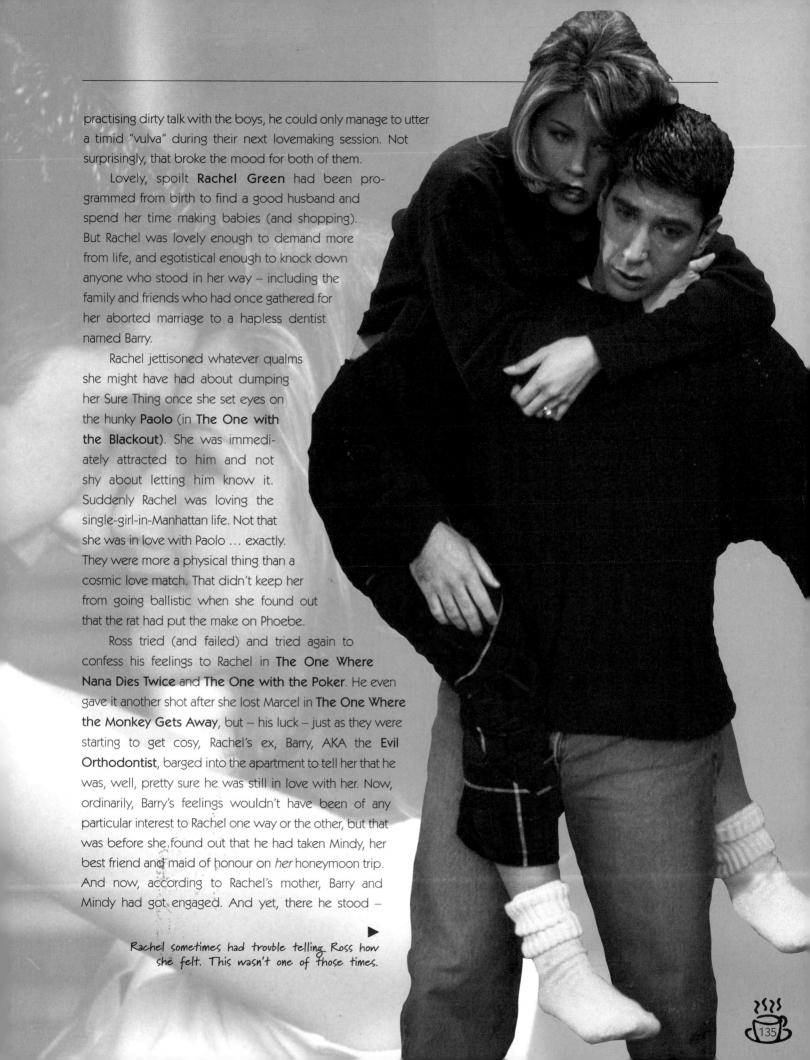

practising dirty talk with the boys, he could only manage to utter a timid "vulva" during their next lovemaking session. Not surprisingly, that broke the mood for both of them.

Lovely, spoilt **Rachel Green** had been programmed from birth to find a good husband and spend her time making babies (and shopping). But Rachel was lovely enough to demand more from life, and egotistical enough to knock down anyone who stood in her way – including the family and friends who had once gathered for her aborted marriage to a hapless dentist named Barry.

Rachel jettisoned whatever qualms she might have had about dumping her Sure Thing once she set eyes on the hunky **Paolo** (in **The One with the Blackout**). She was immediately attracted to him and not shy about letting him know it. Suddenly Rachel was loving the single-girl-in-Manhattan life. Not that she was in love with Paolo … exactly. They were more a physical thing than a cosmic love match. That didn't keep her from going ballistic when she found out that the rat had put the make on Phoebe.

Ross tried (and failed) and tried again to confess his feelings to Rachel in **The One Where Nana Dies Twice** and **The One with the Poker**. He even gave it another shot after she lost Marcel in **The One Where the Monkey Gets Away**, but – his luck – just as they were starting to get cosy, Rachel's ex, Barry, AKA the **Evil Orthodontist**, barged into the apartment to tell her that he was, well, pretty sure he was still in love with her. Now, ordinarily, Barry's feelings wouldn't have been of any particular interest to Rachel one way or the other, but that was before she found out that he had taken Mindy, her best friend and maid of honour on *her* honeymoon trip. And now, according to Rachel's mother, Barry and Mindy had got engaged. And yet, there he stood –

▶

Rachel sometimes had trouble telling Ross how she felt. This wasn't one of those times.

intent on winning her back. Barry had all the right moves in that department: he took her shopping and he made mad, passionate love to her in his dentist's chair. Maybe she did feel something for Barry after all – or so she thought, until Mindy told her that she and Barry had been having an affair during their engagement. This little bombshell left both Rachel and Mindy beyond livid. But after Rachel blew off Barry, Mindy took him back – though maybe that was what she'd had in mind all along.

Ross at last had the opportunity he had been waiting for. And surely he would have made his move – if only he hadn't received an assignment from the museum to retrieve a dinosaur bone from China (in **The One with Ross's New Girlfriend**).

Now it was Rachel's turn to blow it: Chandler let drop that Ross was "totally in love" with her, inspiring her to propose to Ross that they give Them a try. And that would undoubtedly have been welcome news to Ross – if only he had seen Rachel before he hopped on to the aeroplane (wearing his Walkman earphones and oblivious to the world). Oh well. She would just have to tell him when he got back. At least, she would if he hadn't deplaned with Julie, his new girlfriend. Not one to let nature take its course, Rachel did everything she

"No, you hang up ... OK, one, two, three ... Well, you didn't hang up, either ... Come on, you hang up ... You!" — Ross, on the phone with his new girlfriend, Julie

▼

could to sabotage the budding romance. She even got Julie to tell her endless life story to the gang on the very night Ross had planned to consummate their affair (in **The One with Phoebe's Husband**). This time it was Ross's turn to be oblivious to the vibes Rachel was putting out, and he and Julie got closer and closer. Maybe Monica was right, and Rachel was just going to have to "get over it". Getting back into the dating swing of things seemed a logical beginning, so she went out on a date with a friend of a friend who'd just got divorced. But all she did was blather on endlessly to the poor guy about Ross and Julie, while downing one cocktail after another. Her date told her that what she needed was closure. In an attempt to reach that vaunted state, she left Ross a drunken message on his telephone answering machine about how she was "over him". When Ross tried to retrieve his telephone messages from her apartment the next morning, she (literally) jumped on his head and rode him across the room in a frantic attempt to divert his attention. But it was no use; he'd heard it loud and clear. What was this "over him thing" about, he demanded. The reality slowly dawned on him, but it was too huge, too momentous to even contemplate. Come on now ... he was a man with a girlfriend. Later that night, as Rachel was locking up at Central Perk, Ross showed up unannounced to say that even though he'd loved her since the ninth grade, it was too late for them to work things out. "The point is, I don't need this now," he said firmly. He slammed out through the door, but when he looked back, he saw that Rachel had dissolved into tears. He was back in a flash, pulling Rachel into an embrace that would last for, well, until the end of the season anyway.

Of course, there were a few bumps along the way – like when Rachel found Ross's list detailing her virtues and vices versus Julie's. Ross was crushed by Rachel's rejection and, of course, the gang felt badly too. But Rachel felt fine, because she had started dating a new

guy who looked just like Ross (in **The One with Russ**). Not that she could see the resemblance. At first, anyway. But once she did, she promptly dumped him. He still stopped by Central Perk quite a bit, though. One day when he was there, Ross's ex, Julie, happened to come in. Her eyes met Russ's and you could almost see Cupid's arrow ripping through their hearts.

In **The One with the Prom Video** the gang all watched an old home video that Jack Geller had taken on the evening of Monica's senior high school prom. Starring in the opus were the pudgy Monica, the Afro'd Ross, and the pre-nose-job Rachel – who was having a fit because she thought she'd been stood up by her date. At his father's urging, Ross had dashed off to put on his dad's tux and step in as Rachel's knight in shining

On her first date with Michael, Rachel got plastered and called Ross to tell him that she was "over him". ▼

"I thought Jackie Bright (far right), Kevin's dad, was a total pisser in his cameo in The One with Barry and Mindy's Wedding, says Michael Lembeck, who directed the episode. "With the old Borscht Belt guys like Jackie, you just get out of the way and let them do their thing." ▶

Chloe was in the right place at the right time, and Ross went for it.

armour. Predictably, though, by the time he got back downstairs, Rachel and her date were heading out through the door.

Ross may have lost the girl in this video saga, but not in the epilogue. Seeing his well-meaning attempt to come to her rescue all those years ago moved Rachel more than his apologetic words ever could. As the gang watched, she got up and strode slowly and deliberately towards him and kissed him deeply on the lips.

After they returned from their first official date, they drifted towards each other, a dreamy look in their eyes, and then melted into an embrace. That is, they did until Rachel started giggling uncontrollably. She promised to get it together, but by then it was Ross's turn to be spooked. Seeing his frustration, Rachel demanded that he grab her ass. When he shied away, she even tried backing up into his hands, but by then his romantic ardour had totally deflated. It was almost a relief when Ross got an emergency call telling him to report to the museum immediately. Rachel insisted on going with him, even though she was bored to tears. But later Ross took her into the museum's planetarium, where he spun the fake stars in the fake heavens for her amusement.

Although we didn't see exactly what happened next, we had a very good idea – and boy, were we relieved.

Once they were an official couple, Ross (being Ross) pushed Rachel too far, too fast. By **The One with the Giant Poking Device**, he had already decided how many children they were going to have, what sex they would be and in what order they would be born. (Oh yeah, and their names.)

Ross would do anything to make Rachel happy – even if it made her unhappy. He ran himself ragged trying to keep her battling parents apart when they both showed up at her surprise birthday party in **The One with Two Parties**. And he accompanied Rachel to **The One with Barry and Mindy's Wedding** – where she embarrassed both of them by walking down the aisle with the back of her skirt tucked into her panties.

When Rachel couldn't get out of work in time to celebrate their anniversary (in **The One Where Ross and Rachel Take a Break**), Ross took it upon himself to create a candlelit dinner for two right in her office.

The guys never planned for Rachel to show up when they gave Ross the bright idea of comparing his girlfriends in a list. ▼

CONS

RACHEL
spoilt
too into her looks
kind of ditzy
just a waitress
chubby ankles

JULIE
she's not Rachel

◄ Rachel told Mark that if she got involved with him, she would just be doing it to get back at Ross ... so he suggested that they get back at Ross together.

Unfortunately he ended up setting her desk on fire. When she arrived home at the apartment later, Ross was there waiting for an apology. But Rachel felt Ross should apologize to her. No longer a child-woman dependent on others for her survival, Rachel had a great job and, best of all, a discount at Bloomingdale's — and she wanted him to respect and acknowledge it.

Seeing that she wasn't getting anywhere with Ross, Rachel told him that it was time for a break ... from Them. Devastated, he stumbled into a neighbourhood bar where he ran into Chloe, the very sexy girl from the Xerox store. They started to dance, and Chloe asked him if he was married (not that it mattered). As they got closer, Ross got more drunk, and before you could say "copy and collate", he'd woken up with a

►

"I fell asleep. It was 5.30 in the morning and you had rambled on for eighteen pages... FRONT AND BACK!" — Ross

hangover and Chloe in his bed. The next morning, in **The One the Morning After**, Rachel – remorseful about their tiff – went over to his place to tell him that she was so, so sorry. What she didn't know, thank goodness, was that Chloe was still there in his apartment. In fact, she was hiding behind the door. Ross managed to manoeuvre Rachel out before she saw Chloe, but in trying to cover his trail with everyone who had heard the tawdry story, he led Rachel straight to the awful truth. Ross begged and pleaded and told her that he would want her back even if she had slept with Mark, but Rachel wasn't impressed.

They both agreed to cease hostilities for the sake of the group, but even their forced civility cracked when Rachel went out on a date with Mark from work – which made Ross think that he'd been right in being jealous about him (and her) all along. But the truth was that Rachel wasn't into having a thing with Mark. She would only be doing it to get back at Ross, she told Mark.

Even though they were officially Splitsville, it was pretty clear that Ross still cared for Rachel – to everyone but Rachel. But she wouldn't give an inch on the issue of The Break. Phoebe felt so badly for him that she fixed

Everything was moving along quite nicely between Ross and Bonnie ... until Rachel talked her into shaving her head. ▼

Ross was the only one who could see that Tommy the Screamer (guest star Ben Stiller) was a total nut. ▼

thing she wanted to know was how he felt about the letter. When he told her he agreed with everything in it, she was beyond overjoyed.

When Ross did actually read Rachel's tome, he discovered, to his outrage, that she expected him to take full responsibility for causing the break-up by having cheated on her. He didn't say anything about it then, but later, when they were lounging in bed, Rachel complimented him again for being man enough to take the blame. That did it. They rowed and Ross stormed out through the door.

So, it was back to the Dating Game for both Ross and Rachel. And it was back to the old jealousy routine as they tormented each other with accounts of their new romances. Ross, for one, had plenty to brag about because all his dates were incredibly great-looking. But it was never long before things went wrong. **Cheryl** was a knockout blonde scientist. But she was also a secret slob whose apartment was filthy. And then there was **Amanda**, the hot-looking mother of one of Ben's little friends. He thought she had something sexy in mind when she asked him over for the evening. She thought he'd agreed to babysit the boys.

Ross's next girlfriend had everything – beauty, brains and a clean apartment – but she lived two and a half hours north of New York. Much as he wanted to get something going with her (in **The One with the Girl from Poughkeepsie**), he just couldn't handle the commute. That meant he was alone at Christmas. But at least Rachel was too.

him up with a darling girl named Bonnie (in **The One with the Ultimate Fighting Champion**), and he seemed happy for the first time in months. Or he did until Rachel managed to talk her into shaving her head in **The One at the Beach**. By this, the last episode of the third season, Rachel was giving out clear signals to Ross that she wanted him back.

The Friends were still at the beach after a long, long summer break in **The One with the Jellyfish**. Ross had broken up with Bonnie and sent her home to Manhattan in a taxi, and he and Rachel were really, for sure, back together. She just had one itsy-bitsy request before they made it official: that he read a heartfelt eighteen-page letter she has written to him about their break-up. And he would have, if he hadn't been up all night hashing things out with Bonnie and Rachel. The next day, the first

Being alone at Christmas was so sucky, Rachel grumbled to Chandler and Joey, that she was almost tempted to consider a little fling. No problem, Chandler assured her, he would set her up with someone from his office. And, sure enough, when he showed Rachel's photo to his colleagues, he suddenly became the most popular guy at work. But that might have been because he mentioned the Fling Thing when he was pitching her to the guys.

Rachel decided (in **The One with Rachel's Crush**) to take her love life back into her own hands and invite **Joshua** (guest star Tate Donovan), a customer from work, on a date. However, she'd never asked anyone out before, and she wasn't sure how to do it.

Joshua eventually asked Rachel out (in **The One with Joey's Dirty Day**), but she'd already agreed to entertain Emily, her boss's niece who was visiting from England. After everyone else turned her down, she palmed her off on Ross — who was less than thrilled.

This Emily from England was far from charming when she made her entrance into the Friends' lives. In fact, she was plenty crabby. In all fairness, though, she was meeting everyone after having a rotten day … what with the rain, the traffic and New York being New York. And now she'd trekked all the way to Rachel's, only to be told that someone else would be taking her out for the evening. After her little tirade, no one was more surprised than Ross when he ended up falling for her. They had such a wonderful night together that he didn't want it to end. Instead, he took her to a bed-and-breakfast in Vermont for the weekend. When he

▶

They'd only known each other for a few weeks, but, in an impetuous moment, Ross had asked Emily to marry him — and she — even more impetuously — had said yes.

got back to town, he was totally blissed. Emily was wonderful, he said. "I'm finally where you are," he told Rachel — who was so, so not happy for him.

But it wasn't like there weren't problems. The woman Ross was in love with lived in London, baby. At Monica's urging, Ross called Emily as soon as she arrived home and told her he loved her (in **The One with the Free Porn**). With that, Emily turned right around and headed back to New York for another all-too-brief visit. When Emily tried to leave again, Ross got her to stay by asking her to marry him. He was crazy, she told him, and then she said yes. They rushed in to give the gang the news. Rachel, who looked devastated, managed to hug them both and do a reasonably good impression of being happy for them.

Ross and Emily were putting together their guest list for the wedding in **The One with the Invitation**. Ross was going to invite Rachel, but Emily told him she didn't think *she'd* be comfortable with any of her old lovers there. And anyway, there was no way Rachel could bring herself to go to the wedding.

Yet Rachel did go to London — with the express intention of stopping the wedding. But she couldn't go through with it once she saw Ross and Emily having a pre-wedding cuddle. Instead, she just wished him luck. And then Ross said Rachel's name instead of Emily's in his vows. Ross thought it was just a silly mistake. But he couldn't seem to convince Emily. She continued with the ceremony, but she fled from Ross and the reception soon after. Then she had a change of heart and decided to go with him on their honeymoon, but when she got to the airport, she saw Ross boarding the aeroplane with none other than Rachel. That was it. Emily would only consider reconciling with Ross on the condition that he exorcize Rachel from his life: that meant getting rid of anything she'd been near, moving away from the gang, and, most important of all, never seeing Rachel again. Ross knew that would mean breaking up the group, and as much as he wanted Emily back, he just couldn't be responsible for that.

In the meantime, Rachel set her sights on a new guy named **Danny**. The only drawback was his disturbingly intimate relationship with his sister. Ross, who was

Joey demonstrates to Judy and Jack Geller the tricky art of eating steak when standing up.

totally crazed from the news that Emily was getting married, allowed himself to get involved with (Chandler's) Janice. He was horribly uptight about Chandler finding out – but that was before he knew that Chandler was having an intense romance with his sister. Naturally there was no way he and Janice were going to last – but the surprise was that it was Janice who threw him out because she couldn't take his whining any more.

► "Can we just forget this ever happened?" – Ross

Joey and Chandler help Ross "get back on his feet" by talking him into renting a grungy, overpriced apartment instead of staying at their place. ▼

Ross might have had another chance with Emily if he'd returned her call when she left him a message saying that she was having second thoughts about getting married again. But Rachel talked him out of it – for his own good. Not because she was still interested in him romantically. Funny thing though, he didn't seem to get the message.

The last time we saw the two of them at the end of the fifth season, they were lurching out of one of those quickie-wedding chapels in Vegas. Had they actually made their vows? If so, how were they going to feel about it when they sobered up? These were questions that would only be answered in episode one of the sixth season.

Rachel tries to comfort Ross after he receives a package from Emily with 72 long stemmed red roses, one for each day he'd known and loved her, cut up into mulch ... But, at least Monica offered to make pot pourri. ▼

Ross: "Well helloooo, Mrs Ross!"
Rachel: "Well helloooo, Mr Rachel!"
▼

DAVID SCHWIMMER
PROFILE

David Schwimmer's undeniable appeal led critics to single him out as the show's first break-out star. Somewhere along the way, he also became a pin-up boy – although he would be the first to admit that he's an unlikely heart-throb. And yet, *Playgirl* magazine voted him one of 1995's Ten Sexiest Men.

No one could have anticipated the frenzy *Friends* would stir up, least of all David Schimmer. Sidestepping his considerable contributions to the show, he instead attributed the show's success to its ability to capitalize on a universal longing for family. "This kind of solid support group is something everyone wants in their lives," he said.

David continues to believe that *Friends* has tapped into an evolving notion of friendship. "In my parents' generation, people have only one or two close friends," he observes, "whereas I literally have twenty really close friends who are constantly calling, crashing, or hanging out at my house at any given time. Not that we set out to, but I guess you could say that my age group has sort of reinvented family on its own terms. And I can't think of another show that's shown it the way *Friends* has."

Happily, David Schwimmer is the product of a long and successful marriage. Both his parents are high-powered Los Angeles attorneys and he grew up in a well-to-do, close-knit family. But, even though he was a fortunate son, Schwimmer remembers himself as being something of a misfit as a child. "My big sister, Ellie, was the good one," he says. "I was the rebellious kid, always in trouble. I was constantly getting suspended from school – that's what happens when you're the class clown."

Ross Geller has always been a Good Boy. To his mother he was a prince, and to his father he was a "mensch". However, it's pretty obvious that everyone else thought he was a total nerd – especially when he was growing up. He was the guy in high school who everyone else cheated off. He was also the guy who told the teacher on the cheaters – for their own good.

Ross started getting a little cooler in college – where it was okay to be smart and make high marks. It was also there that he started his own rock band. But it's not like he used his higher profile to get girls. That wouldn't have been nice. He stuck with his girlfriend and married her right after graduation, and he would've stayed that way for life if, well, you know ... Fortunately for us, it is now Ross's turn to be crazy: to do all the rash things he never allowed himself to do as a young man – like sleeping around and wearing leather pants. In fact, there's no telling what he'll do next. He might even marry Rachel.

But school wasn't nearly as funny once David moved into the stratified atmosphere of Beverly Hills High. "I was always bigger than my friends until high school. Suddenly everyone else shot up, and I didn't grow. I was short and pudgy, and it turned me into a less-than-confident loser." David felt out of place in the school that was the inspiration for *Beverly Hills 90210*. However, it was in high school that the acting bug bit David after he played a part in *West Side Story* alongside one of his best buddies (still), *The Single Guy's* Jonathan Silverman.

For a time David considered studying law or medicine, but a summer course in theatre held at Chicago's Northwestern University sold him on acting. He attended Northwestern for four years, graduating in 1988 with a BSc in

"When we get to work, we check our egos at the door and just concentrate on coming up with the best jokes, giving each other healthy criticism or suggestions and, basically, just having a blast together."
– *David Schwimmer*

Like any normal kid growing up in the seventies, Ross Geller wore some pretty silly-looking get-ups. (And they have come back to haunt him in flashback episodes.) Nowadays though, he is most often seen in the fashionably rumpled designer threads he wears on the job at the Museum of Natural History. Of course, when he's hanging out at home or at Central Perk, he's casual in baggy jeans and T-shirts. But unlike the rest of his habitually broke friends, Ross has a good bit of money jangling around in the pockets of his Italian trousers – which means that Debra McGuire can dress him in expensive suits and separates – like the soft suede jacket and layered separates above.

speech/theatre. He then used his savings to co-found The Lookingglass Theater Company in Chicago with a group of fellow graduates. After returning to L.A. he landed only one job in six months so he returned to Chicago again to work in the theatre. Two years later, he tried L.A. again and this time snagged recurring roles on *LA Law*, *The Wonder Years* and *NYPD Blue* in which he played the memorable vigilante 4B.

If the role of Ross seems custom made for Schwimmer, that's because it quite literally was. Marta Kauffman and David Crane, the show's creators, remembered him from a past audition and wrote Ross for the voice they couldn't get out of their heads. And, in fact, Schwimmer was the only cast member offered his part without an audition. But while the others may have been sure they'd signed on to a hit (or so they say now), David Schwimmer was less than convinced. "I figured *Friends* was just another temporary thing," he confesses, "I was sleeping on a futon in a friend's living room in Chicago only two months before I filmed the pilot."

David Schwimmer sees himself first and foremost as a character actor – even when he's playing a leading man. As a highly trained stage actor, David is fascinated by what can be conjured up during the process of working on a role. "We do our most interesting work on the rehearsal set," he observes of the *Friends* cast. "That's where we bring things to life that aren't necessarily there on paper. For me, it's a process of making a story ring true emotionally. The writers work at night, but during the day the actors own the set. I sometimes get the feeling that people think we just lounge around on the set all day, but nothing could be further from the truth. We're constantly

"David has the craziest fans," says Courteney Cox. "When he goes out, you'd think The Beatles arrived."

In The One with All the Resolutions, Ross finally got up the nerve to buy himself the pair of black leather pants he'd always wanted. And he looked great in them too. It's just that they were hot – and tight – and they chafed in a very personal place. Unfortunately, he only realized all this after he'd gone over to a date's house to watch TV. He got a little relief when he took the pants off in the bathroom. But then he couldn't get them back on. In his desperation, he called Joey for help – who suggested using baby oil, then talcum powder as lubricants. By the time he finished, the stuff on his legs had turned to paste. By now he'd been in the bathroom for a long, long time.

working to help each other come up with the most original way of doing things. We rely on directors to point the cameras in the right direction, but we have to depend on our own instincts about our characters.

"Ross has a political bent similar to my own," David muses. "He's kind of a conservative liberal in that he's open enough to accept a gay relationship between his ex-wife and her lover. But he's also a traditionalist in that he believes in family values – you know, man and wife and family – and working hard all your life." As complicated and contradictory as these qualities are, Schwimmer wants even more from his character. "I've thought a lot about this," he says, "and what I've realized is that just as I have changed in the last several years, it's inevitable that Ross would, too.

David still relies on the often painfully candid opinions of the members of his theatre company. For instance, the general consensus among

his support group was that his first big-screen starring role in *The Pallbearer* was too similar to Ross. "I was perplexed by that," he says now. "I thought I'd done my homework."

Because David Schwimmer's first love is the theatre, it's not surprising that he believes that working in front of a studio audience has given him the biggest thrill while doing *Friends*. "With live theatre you have the feeling of the audience being with you," he says, "and with *Friends* you have an audience that has been with you for five years! Like, when we were shooting Ross and Rachel's break-up – to feel the studio audience there with you, knowing what was at stake between the characters … I've never experienced anything like it. It was so overwhelming that when it was over, and both of us were crying, it took a long time for me to get my bearings, I was so shaken." Thanks to David Schwimmer, millions of viewers felt the same way.

The in-laws were fighting, the bride was freaking and, as usual, poor Ross was right in the middle.

THE FIFTH SEASON

What could Emily do? It's not as if she could deck Ross right then and there. "Do go on," she told the registrar without a trace of pique. Ross did go on, too – taking special care to enunciate the name Em-i-ly the next time around. They exchanged rings and were pronounced husband and wife (in **The One After Ross Says "Rachel"**). Ross tried to kiss his bride, but she managed to dodge him. Then, on their walk down the aisle, she shook him off when he tried to take her arm. "Just keep smiling," she hissed as they passed the bewildered guests.

At the reception the gang cringed outside Ross and Emily's room as they screamed at each other. Later Rachel asked Ross – in a roundabout way – just what it had meant when he said her name. "It didn't mean anything!" he yelled in the direction of Emily's (now locked) door. Funny, Rachel told him, but Emily's retreat made her think back to her own wedding – and how she had locked

▲ "You know when I locked myself in the bathroom at my wedding?" Rachel reminisced as she, Ross and Joey waited outside Emily's locked door at the wedding reception. "It was 'cause I was trying to pop the window out of the frame and get the hell out of there."

► High-fives all around! The gang is gonna take Phoebe for a weekend in Atlantic City to make up for leaving her behind on the London trip. (That is, they were until her waters broke a split second later.)

Monica: "Welcome to an adult relationship."
Chandler: "We're in a relationship?"
Monica: "I'm afraid so."

herself in the bathroom and escaped out of the window. Ross froze. What if Emily …? He crashed through the door to their room and sure enough the window was open and Emily was gone.

Thinking Emily might reconsider and go with him on their honeymoon to Greece, Ross went to the airport – where, of course, he ran into Rachel, who was trying to get on a stand-by flight to New York. Rachel convinced him that he should go to Greece and take some time to think about what happened and what he felt. Maybe he should, he said, and why didn't she come with him? "Yes, I can do that!" she said happily. That *would* be when Emily showed up – just as Ross and Rachel were boarding. "No-no-no-no," Ross sputtered – knowing what she must think. Aghast, Emily turned and ran. Ross chased her through the airport. Meanwhile, on board the plane Rachel ordered a white wine spritzer for him from the flight attendant.

By **The One with all the Kissing**, Rachel had just returned from Greece, where she'd put Ross and

Emily's honeymoon package to good use, or so she told Ross. But once he had gone, Rachel told everyone what her fabulous vacation had really been like. "Ross abandoned me," she said. "And I had to stay in their honeymoon suite, with people coming up to me and saying, 'Oh Mrs Geller, why you cry?'" Be that as it may,

MISTER BOFFO By Joe Martin

Rachel still wanted to tell Ross that she loved him. "Wow," he said in response. "I'm not sure what to do with that right now." After laughing hysterically at his stricken expression, she asked him to kinda just forget that she'd ever said what she did.

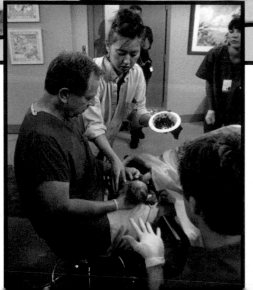

▲ "It seems like only yesterday that I was talking to you in that petrie dish," Phoebe tells the babies before she turns them over to Frank Jr and Alice.

◄ Chandler absent-mindedly gives Monica a big, wet good-bye kiss as Rachel looks on in disbelief.

Prop diva Marjorie Coster-Praytor touches up one of the newborn dolls with baby goo, so that it can look — in Frank Jr's words — "totally gross".

In this October 1998 US cover story on Jennifer Aniston, Courteney Cox said, "Jennifer's a real girl's girl. Guys love her, but women really love her and are not threatened by her. It's a really good sign when someone has a lot of good girlfriends."

100TH EPISODE PARTY

What's better than a wedding, bar mitzvah, and tailgate party all rolled into one? The party for The Hundredth Episode of *Friends*, that's what. Reaching this number is a landmark event in the life of any sitcom because it ensures that it will live on for ever in syndication eternity. On hand to celebrate the joyous event with the cast and crew were former guest stars, star boyfriends, past directors and TV execs galore. Champagne glasses in hand, they wandered the Warner Bros. backlot – which had been extravagantly transformed into a New York street for the occasion. At the centre of the festivities were the core members of the *Friends* family – all of whom said a few words to the gathered multitudes. And Matthew Perry who said a few more (funny) words than anyone else. The party took place following a show taping and the beginning of a three-week long hiatus, so the crowd felt no guilt in boogying till the sun came up in the hazy Burbank sky.

Joey: "Why don't you like PBS, Phoebe?"
Phoebe: "Right after my mom killed herself, I was in this really bad place, you know, personally, so I just thought it would make me feel better if I wrote to Sesame Street 'cause they were so nice when I was a little kid — and no one ever wrote back!" ▼

Meanwhile, Chandler and Monica had decided to break their "no sex in New York rule" – seeing as Chandler was still on London time. Now the problem became trying to keep the others from finding out about their budding relationship. When Chandler absent-mindedly gave Monica a big, wet good-bye kiss in front of Rachel and Phoebe, he tried to cover by kissing them in the same ardent way. What was that, Rachel demanded after he left. "It must be some sort of European-good-bye thing he picked up in London," Monica improvised.

19 October 1998 Courteney Cox didn't talk to People magazine for this cover story, but that didn't keep it from ferreting out most of the particulars about her engagement to her Scream co-star, David Arquette.

Holy Matt-rimony! Lauer's model wedding

OCTOBER 19, 1998

Darryl Strawberry's brave battle

People weekly

Today's Matt Lauer & Annette Roque

David and Courteney in Jane

Courteney Cox
ENGAGED!
Forever single on *Friends*, she finds love with *Scream* costar David Arquette

PEOPLE Weekly is a registered trademark of Time Inc. used with permission.

Kevin S. Bright with his children Justin and Zachary.

◀Will Ross find the key to all his problems in the wisdom of the Magic Eight Ball? Ask again later.

The group decided to take Phoebe to Atlantic City to make up for leaving her behind (in **The One Hundredth**), but just as they were heading out, her waters broke. She tried to ignore it, but her babies – all three of them – wouldn't co-operate. The gang checked her into the hospital, but there was some disturbing news awaiting her there; her doctor had slipped in the shower and wouldn't be able to make it for her delivery. Ross tried to find another replacement, but the next candidate looked about twelve. "Go away, little boy," Phoebe told him, making him cry – which Frank Jr thought was very cool.

Frank Jr was ecstatic at the birth, running out to the waiting room to announce each new arrival. Alice, who'd had to drive in from Delaware, arrived shortly after the third baby. "We have our babies!" Frank Jr told her ecstatically as they hugged and then fell to the floor in a passionate embrace.

Phoebe had made Frank Jr and Alice happy with her selfless act, and Joey was into altruism, too, he told her. He was going to donate his services to PBS to host a pledge telethon. Phoebe took a dim view of anything connected with PBS because of a long-standing grudge she held against the network. It seems that she had written to *Sesame Street* after her mother committed suicide, thinking that someone there – Big Bird, maybe – would respond with some comforting words. But nobody wrote back. "All I got was a lousy key-chain, and by then I was living in a box," she ranted. "I didn't need *keys*!" Joey felt he was performing a "selfless" gesture by hosting the telethon. Phoebe didn't buy that either … he was just trying to get on camera. Joey

"I love it when there are children on the set," says executive producer Marta Kauffman. "Lisa brings her baby a lot and our props mistress had a baby, and she's on the set. It's great! It keeps women interested in working, because they don't feel that their lives are as divided. I mean it's hard enough to have to separate from your child as much as we do. There are some times when it's too stressful, but my kids usually come on show nights. And sometimes if I'm working a late night during the week – like on a Thursday before the show – they'll come and spend some time with me. It makes for a wonderful atmosphere. I'll go up to give notes, and they'll scuttle along behind me and sort of hang there and listen. They've even been known to give me notes."

Marta Kauffman with her children Anna and Sam.

challenged her to come up with a good deed that didn't have some sort of ulterior motive – even if it was just making the good-deed-doer feel good about themselves. The selfless act she came up with was using money she'd been saving to buy a hamster to call Joey and pledge 200 dollars to the telethon. Lo and behold, her pledge put the network over its goal and gave Joey some major face time on camera.

Meanwhile, Ross spent all his spare time calling Emily's relatives in a desperate attempt to track her down. Finally Emily called him herself to order him to stop badgering her family. Seizing his chance, Ross pleaded with her to reconcile with him. Miraculously, she agreed. There was only one condition: he must never see Rachel again. When Rachel heard about Emily's ultimatum (in **The One with the Kips**), she began to worry that it wouldn't only be Ross she was losing, but the rest of the gang, too. Just like Kip, Monica's old boyfriend, who'd been a fully-fledged member of the group until the two of them

▶

Phoebe: "I don't know what I'm going to do about the coat."
Joey: "I'll take it."
Phoebe: "That might work."
— Phoebe, on trying to find a home for her dead-animal coat

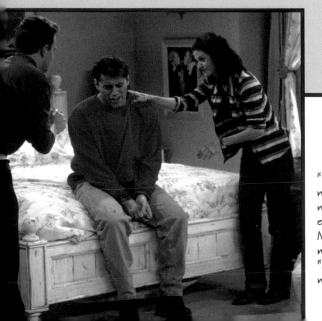

"We just don't want to deal with telling everyone," Monica pleaded with Joey. "Promise you won't tell."

Courteney Cox did make-overs on a Racine, Wisconsin police officer; a Brooklyn New York Internet developer; and a bank teller from Portland, Oregon in the December 1998 issue of Marie Claire. (Really.)

had broken up. But Ross, quite reasonably, told Rachel that since he was the one who was making The Choice, he should be the one to step back.

Meanwhile, Monica and Chandler were closer than ever. They'd even contrived a plan to sneak off together for a weekend in Atlantic City. Several days later the hotel left a message with Joey saying that Chandler had left an eyelash curler in his room. The reality of the situation dawned on him later, when he heard Monica mention that she'd lost her eyelash curler. As he started to freak, Chandler and Monica wrestled him out of the room before he could blurt out their secret.

Of course, Joey didn't have a problem with Monica and Chandler being together. But that didn't mean he wanted to see them touching and kissing and stuff like that. If he was going to pretend he didn't know about them, he told them, they would have to pretend there was nothing to know about — at least in front of him.

Meanwhile, to help Ross make the break with Rachel, Emily wanted him to move uptown and sublet her cousin's apartment. "Emily thinks Ross has Rachel cooties?" Joey asked after hearing about Emily's anti-Rachel mandate. "I'm not happy about this either," Monica answered, "but if Ross says he's happy, then

▲ "Well, I guess that's it. My marriage is over." – Ross

"I thought (Courteney) was going to be celebrity-ish. But she wasn't at all." – Lisa Kudrow

Danny Cruz (boom operator) and Don Howard (utility) watch the action from the catwalk.

"Lisa Kudrow is the smartest person I know." – Courteney Cox

we're just going to have to keep our feelings about Emily to ourselves." But Joey was carrying around more secrets than he could handle – and it was inevitable that he would let one slip. So while they were all helping Ross move, he suddenly blurted out, "It's not right what Emily wants you to do. We all hate Emily!" Monica jumped in to smooth things over, saying that they *all* didn't *hate* Emily. But, Chandler added delicately, they did think she was being a little unreasonable. Especially about Rachel. But they needn't have worried. Rachel was already hot on the trail of a new boyfriend.

Rachel and Monica had been frightened by a "crazy-eyed, hairy beast-man" in the storage room of their apartment building. But that was no beast-man, it was a guy named Danny – who had just returned from a four-month trek in the Andes. The women apologized profusely for savagely bug-bombing him when they ran into him, but Danny wasn't buying it. The next time Rachel saw Danny, he was all cleaned up and looking like a really cute guy –

Monica: "Look, I'm not happy about this either, but if Ross says he's happy, then we'll just have to keep our feelings about Emily to ourselves. Are you cool with that?"
Joey: "No, but I'm an actor, I'll act cool." ▼

which made it easier to apologize again. But this time around he was even more rude. "I would never have fogged you if you hadn't looked so, so ..." she tried to explain. "Absolutely," he said snidely, "some people are just into appearances." Now he had gone too far. But that didn't stop her from going for a pizza with him.

Rachel returned to the apartment to find everyone gathered for dinner, but instead of joining them she said she would rather just stay in her room. After all, if Emily knew she and Ross were together, she would have a coronary. But Ross demanded that she sit down and eat. Later Emily called looking for Ross, and Joey said something stupid that let her know that Rachel was there. Ross took the telephone and walked out on the balcony so he could get yelled at in private. "This marriage isn't going to work if you can't trust me," he told her. "Can

After Ross lost the apartment he and Emily were going to sublet together, he moved in with Chandler and Joey — and proceeded to drive them buggy by constantly telling them to "quiet down" as if they were eight-year-olds and worse, taping over a Baywatch episode with a show about bugs.

you?" Nope, she couldn't. And that was that.

Ross's marriage was over by **The One Where Ross Moves In**. And to make things even more bleak, Emily's cousin had kicked him out of the apartment they were going to sublet together, so he was going to have to find a new place and get all his stuff back from Gunther. In the meantime, he moved in with Chandler and Joey and proceeded to drive them crazy. He taped over Joey's *Baywatch* episode with a show about bugs. And then he changed their answering-machine message to one of him singing "We Will Call You Back" to the tune of "We Will Rock You". Things got so bad that the guys talked him into renting a really tiny, really grungy apartment just to get rid of him. But when the landlord called them for references, Chandler felt so guilty about pushing him into a place where he was

This is what they looked like — Thanksgiving 1987!

bound to be miserable that he told him that Ross was a pimp.

The Friends gathered for **The One with All the Thanksgivings** to share memories of Thanksgivings past. Their trip down memory lane took Chandler back to the year his parents told him that they were getting a divorce and his father was having an affair with the house-boy. The mocking voice of the triumphant house-boy still rang in his ears, as he taunted him with, "More turkey, Mr Chandler?" Phoebe's most vivid memory took her back to a previous life in 1862 when she was a nurse ministering to the wounded during the Civil War. Next came Joey's story about the time he had the bright idea of putting Monica's huge uncooked turkey on his head so that he could scare Chandler. Of course the turkey got stuck on his head, and the inside smelled really bad.

Monica was next. Flash back to Thanksgiving 1987 and the now-familiar fat Monica and pre-nose-job

The '98–99 writing staff take time out to pose with the cast.

"Of course it smells really bad ... you have your head up a dead animal ass," Phoebe tells Joey when he gets stuck in Monica's Thanksgiving turkey.

▶ Monica told Chandler that she loves the way the cold steel of the carving knife feels against her body.

Eat your heart out, Crockett and Tubbs. Ross and Chandler are looking muy macho in their slick Miami Vice threads in the Friends Thanksgiving flashback. ▼

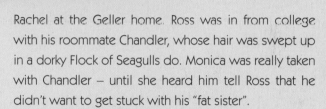

Rachel at the Geller home. Ross was in from college with his roommate Chandler, whose hair was swept up in a dorky Flock of Seagulls do. Monica was really taken with Chandler – until she heard him tell Ross that he didn't want to get stuck with his "fat sister".

The following Thanksgiving Ross brought Chandler home for the holiday weekend again. But this time he wasn't about to blow Monica off, because she'd slimmed down to almost nothing and looked absolutely gorgeous. She lured him into the kitchen with the intention of humiliating him as he'd humiliated her, but the next thing we saw was Chandler being wheeled into the ER on a stretcher – with Rachel and the Gellers following close behind. Apparently Monica had somehow ended up lopping off Chandler's toe. Thinking quickly, she had brought the severed appendage with her, so it could be

She helped Monica put on the weight. Costume designer Debra McGuire with Courteney Cox in her famous fat suit.

"When Courteney first showed up on the set in her fat make-up and costume," remembers writer Alexa Junge, "she walked by Matthew Perry and said, 'Hey.' He had no idea who she was."

reattached. But when the doctor opened the neatly-wrapped package she took from her bag, he found that it contained a carrot instead of a toe.

Flash forward to Thanksgiving Present and a mortified Chandler saying to Monica, "That's why I lost my toe … because I called you *fat*?" Monica said she was sorry, sorry, sorry. That was fine, Chandler said, but that didn't "bring back the Little Piggy that cried all the way home".

Speaking of bad behaviour, the gang was used to Ross's little diatribes, but he was starting to scare his co-workers at the museum, who had taken to calling him "Mental Geller". Things became so bad that his boss insisted he see a psychiatrist about his excessive rage. Ross might have been all right with that, if he hadn't then discovered that it was his boss who'd eaten his leftover Thanksgiving turkey sandwich. That threw him into yet another tantrum that earned him an involuntary leave-of-absence from work. But the good news was that when he went to see the shrink, she gave him a little pill that made him forget about work and his sandwich and pretty much everything else.

Meanwhile, Joey was taking the rap for the debris left behind by Monica and Chandler. First he took the blame for a pair of Chandler's errant underpants, which showed up under a cushion on Monica's sofa. And then he had to shave his legs after Rachel found Monica's razor in the guys' bathroom. "That's it," Joey told them. "I'm not covering up for you any more." They begged him to help just a little longer. OK, Joey relented, but they had to be more careful. And they were – until the night when Joey returned home with a new girlfriend to find candles and a videotape camera in the living-room. "I can't believe you thought you were going to video-tape us having sex on the first date," Joey's date said indignantly and then made for the stairs. Unfortunately

▲ "If anyone's a sex addict here, it's Monica. She has been trying to get me back in the sack ever since London." — Joey

for Joey, Rachel happened to overhear this exchange in the hall. "What are you … sick?" she demanded. "I'm Joey," he answered dejectedly. "I'm disgusting." But he got his revenge when Rachel found a photo of Monica naked in the guys' apartment, and accused him of being a peeping tom. All right, he would just have to admit it, he said a bit too happily, he'd been having sex with Monica. Yes, it had started in London. And what did

"Did you mean it when you said I was the best one?" Matt LeBlanc confers with Kevin S. Bright.

Monica have to say for herself? "I'm Monica," she said dejectedly. "I'm disgusting."

Meanwhile, Rachel wasn't exactly making much headway with Danny (in **The One with the Inappropriate Sister**). Tired of listening to her convoluted Danny strategies, Monica took it upon herself to ask Danny out on Rachel's behalf. And it worked. "I'm really glad Monica asked us out," Rachel told Danny when they returned from their night together. Oh, and by the way, who was that very attractive woman she'd seen him with on the bus that day? That was his sister, Krista, who was in town visiting.

Rachel would soon discover that Danny and Krista had an unusually close relationship. They were constantly wrestling and tickling and, well, touching each other in a very intimate way. Rachel didn't have brothers, so she couldn't really say, but their relationship

▶ Phoebe: "Is that a new suede jacket? It looks really expensive."
Monica: "Yes, Phoebe ... but this is all I have."
— Phoebe guilt trips Monica into contributing to her Christmas fund

'Tis the Season of Giving

Par-tay! Monica told Rachel that she'd planned a fun Friday night of organizing photos.

"Ross is our Job. He's had the hardest trip of anybody, starting with his wife telling him that she was a lesbian and their marriage was over. What I love is how he rises above it all – that he's always triumphant, emotionally. And David is so funny playing all that." – David Crane

▲ Joey: "All right, Phoebs.
I'm ready for my first lesson on the guitar."
Phoebe: "OK, but, oh no, don't touch the guitar!"

seemed a little weird to her. The others agreed as they watched Krista energetically wiping a stain off the crotch of his trousers. "You seem to have a very special bond with Krista," Rachel began — as she attempted to break things off with Danny gently. He fumed. Why was it women got so crazy about him and his sister, he groused. He told her he thought they could have something special — and indeed, they might have had, if only Krista hadn't picked that very moment to call Danny in for his bath.

No more Danny meant that Rachel was going to be on her own as the New Year's Day holiday approached (in **The One with All the Resolutions**). And, of course, Ross was alone, too. But neither had any intention of letting that get them down. There was a new year dawning and everyone intended to make some real changes in their lives. Ross made a pledge to pleasure himself by doing something he'd never done before. In his case, that meant wearing a pair of tight, black leather trousers. Phoebe's aspirations were a little more high flown: she wanted to pilot a commercial jet. Ross bet Chandler 50 dollars that he couldn't control his

▲ Joey: "I thought I was getting better, so on my way home I stopped at the guitar store."
Phoebe: "So, did you touch any of the guitars while you were there? ... Did you?"
Joey: "No."
Phoebe: "Give me your hands ... (smelling) Strings, pick! Do you want to learn how to play guitar? Then don't touch one!"

sarcastic mouth for even a week. Chandler took that bet, but he was sorry he had done so when Ross showed up later in his funky black leather trousers.

For his resolution, Joey wanted to learn how to play the guitar so that at least one of those "special skills" listed on his resumé would actually be true. Now that particular goal was something Phoebe could help him with. But Joey had a little trouble with her unorthodox teaching method – which required not touching the guitar.

Chandler told Monica that the reason he was so cute was that his grandfather was Swedish and his grandmother was a "tiny little bunny".

Monica challenged Rachel to kick her nasty gossip habit. Of course, that would be when she discovered that Monica and Chandler were having a Thing. There was simply no way she could keep this piece of news to herself – resolution or no resolution. She ran across the hall to tell Joey her gossip, but he didn't want to keep any more secrets, thank you. He started singing at the top of his voice so that he wouldn't hear her, but he could only do that for so long. Oh that, he said when she finally got through to him, yeah, he knew all about it.

Monica discovered a whole new side to Chandler in **The One with Chandler's Work Laugh** – like that he was a real suck-up at work. When she went with him to a company party she discovered that the Work Chandler was constantly toadying up to his boss and even had a bogus blowhard laugh. Monica didn't want to hang out with a "snivelling work-weasel guy", she told him during dinner at his boss's house, when she could be hanging out with her boyfriend whom she respected. Chandler was stung so deeply by her remark that he didn't laugh at the next stupid joke his boss made. Seeing the boss's testy reaction,

▶

"That is just so funny." Monica joins Chandler in his "work laugh".

Monica took pity on the poor guy and quickly bailed him out. She pretended to explain the joke to him – and then they did a fake laugh together.

Rachel never stopped trying to trick or tantalize Monica into telling her the truth about Chandler, but Monica always managed to sidestep her questions. Fed up, Rachel marched across the hall to confront the two of them with what she knew, but as she hovered outside Chandler's bedroom door she overheard Monica saying how much she hated keeping her in the dark. Touched, she decided to cancel the confrontation bit, but as she turned to tiptoe out she knocked over a lamp. Monica – dressed in a tank top and shorts – came rushing out of the bedroom. Improvizing quickly (and lamely), she told Rachel that she was, uh, in Chandler's bedroom because she had taken a new job cleaning his apartment. Rachel sweetly pretended to believe her. "Boy, is she gullible," Chandler said after she had gone.

Meanwhile, Ross got the unsettling news that Emily was getting married. He was so bereft that he ended up

seeking romantic solace with none other than ("oh my god") Janice. Ross felt that Janice, who was also divorced with children, understood his pain in a way no one else could. Yes, Janice understood all right. She understood that Ross was so overcome with self-pity about lesbians and highly-strung British girls that he couldn't seem to talk about anything else.

Phoebe's grandmother died in **The One with Joey's Bag,** but Phoebe said it wasn't so bad, because she was sure she would be visiting all the time. Naturally she went to her sister Ursula's apartment to invite her to the memorial service (which was going to be in 3D). But Ursula had been under the impression that their grandmother had died five years ago, and she didn't want to get herself all upset again. Ursula missed out on a very special unannounced guest – their runaway father, Frank Buffay. Typically, Frank tried to run away yet again after Phoebe reacted so dramatically to his name. But Phoebe wasn't about to let Frank disappear out of her life before she got a chance to ask him a few questions. Using a fake name, she lured him to Central Perk with the story that her grandmother had left him something in her will.

▲ Phoebe had a few questions for her runaway father, Frank Buffay before he ran away again – like had his marriage ended in the total abandonment of his wife and her two children? And if so, what was the reason for said abandonment? Could it be that he was just a totally selfish, bad, bad man?

▲ OK, so maybe it looks a little feminine, but Joey loves the new bag Rachel got him from Bloomingdale's because he can carry everything in it – even a sandwich.

"There's no screaming and yelling on our show. I mean, I've never seen an actor throw a tantrum on our stage. And I think that's unusual because, ultimately, just like a normal human being, things get to you. But I've never seen an actor storm off the stage on *Friends*. I've never heard anybody say, 'Fuck you'."
– Kevin S. Bright

"So, what did Frances leave me?" he asked, getting right down to business. Phoebe told him that she'd left him, uh, a lipstick – the one in her purse. But before they got into that, she said, she had to ask him some questions – like had his marriage ended in the total abandonment of his wife and her two children? Flustered and spooked, Frank answered with a question of his own: would she be willing to give a note to his ex-wife, Lily?

▲
"She would have liked that." Phoebe threw a 3D memorial service for her grandmother.

She couldn't do that, she told him, because Lily had been dead for seventeen years. What? He couldn't believe that she was gone. "If she wasn't," Phoebe told him, "then cremating her was a big mistake." But what about the girls, he asked. Well, Ursula was a waitress living in Soho, and Phoebe was sitting right in front of him on the couch. "In my defence," he said shakily, "I was a lousy father." But Phoebe wasn't through with him yet.

"We had a big turnover in our writing and production staff between years one and two," says Friends producer Todd Stevens. "Believe it or not people left us to go to shows where they wouldn't have to work so hard. They thought: "Ah, it's just a sitcom!"

Friends co-creator David Crane and his lover, Jeffrey Klarik at "The One Hundredth" fete.

Life had been an emotional roller-coaster for Phoebe of late, and she had more stomach-churning plunges ahead in **The One Where Everybody Finds Out**. She actually went blind (just for a second) when she saw Monica and Chandler doing it from the window of Ugly Naked Guy's apartment. She and Rachel had gone there with Ross, who was hoping to rent it. Rachel shushed her, explaining that they couldn't let Ross know what was going on. But, wait a minute – had Rachel known all this time? Yep, she had … and Joey too. Phoebe could understand why Chandler and Monica

would want to keep Ross in the dark, but not *her*. But if they wanted to play that game, she could play too. "Every time they say they're doing laundry," Phoebe proposed to Rachel, "we'll just give them a bunch of our laundry to do too." Rachel thought that was a stellar idea. Joey, on the other hand, didn't want to get involved in any more intrigue, thank you. OK, so Phoebe would just have to smoke out the fakers by making them so uncomfortable that they would have to come clean. For Phoebe that meant only one thing – using her sexual allure. "Watch … and learn", she instructed Rachel as she went off to torture Chandler into telling her the truth.

Suddenly, sultry, Phoebe squeezed his big, strong man-muscles and told him that she hadn't been with anyone in a long, long time …

Phoebe kept coming on to Chandler – and eventually even Monica could see it. Especially when she pinched his bottom. "Oh my god,

▲ Chandler: "What's going on?"
Phoebe: "I think it's just, you know, that I haven't been with a guy in so long and you know how sometimes you're looking for something, and you don't even see that it's right there in front of you sipping coffee."

she knows about us," Monica told him later, "and she's trying to freak us out … that's the only explanation for it." Chandler rushed over to confront Joey with their suspicions. Joey was relieved. Finally he could stop with the secrets. Not so fast, Chandler and Monica told him. Now it was their turn to have fun with Phoebe. Chandler invited Phoebe to come over and feel his biceps "and maybe more". Of course, Rachel knew there was no way Chandler would betray Monica with Phoebe, so it was her turn to confront Joey. Yes-yes-yes, they knew. Everyone – except Ross – knew about everything. Oh yeah, and Chandler and Monica didn't know that Phoebe and Rachel knew that they knew. The question now was who would give in first? Phoebe turned up the heat on her seduction routine, telling Chandler she was really looking forward to having sexual intercourse with him. She then did an artistic dance and showed him her bra. "Come here," Chandler said weakly, "I'm very happy we're going to have all the sex." But he totally lost his cool when it was time actually to kiss her. "I can't," he

▲ "I'd say from the look of it that our naked buddy is moving out. Aw, I'm gonna miss that big old squishy butt." — Rachel

◄ "I thought you guys were doing it. I didn't know you were in love!" — Phoebe

◄ "Instead of just running away from new emotional attachments," says Matthew Perry, "Chandler is willing to give him and Monica a shot. He's always been sort of a slightly exaggerated form of me anyway, so maybe now we're catching up to being the same."

sobbed. "Why?" Phoebe asked innocently. "Because I'm in love with Monica!" he answered. Phoebe was thrilled: she'd known that he and Monica were doing it, she told him, but she hadn't known they were actually in love. But they still had to keep it from Ross. He was just too crazy to handle it now. There was Emily … and work … and the fact that he didn't have anywhere to live yet.

Rachel encouraged Ross to bond with Ugly Naked Guy over something they had in common. So, he went over and got naked with him – and that was all it took. Ross was so thrilled that he took his boss over to his new place so that he could see that he'd finally pulled himself together. Impressed, his boss told him the time had come for him

Ross's puny basket of mini-muffins hadn't even made a dent in the glut of big-ticket bribes Ugly Naked Guy had received from people hoping to sublet his apartment. So Rachel encouraged him to go over and bond with UNG over something they had in common.

to return to his old job at the museum. But just then Ross happened to look out of the window and saw Chandler and Monica doing *it*. Apoplectic, he started screaming, *"Get off my sister!"* at the top of his voice – as his boss slowly backed out of the apartment.

Ross charged over to Monica's and tried to break down the door. Chandler kissed Monica good-bye and then he tried to climb out of the window to "go on the lam". But Monica stayed cool. She let Ross in and tried acting as if nothing was wrong. "I thought you were my best friend," Ross shouted at Chandler. "This is my sister!" Chandler jumped in quickly to defend himself. "Look, we're not just messing around here," he said. "I *love* her." Monica told him gently that she

▲ "Good evening, sir. My name is Ross Geller, and I'm one of the people who applied for your apartment. I'm sorry, but I can't help but notice that you're naked … and I applaud that!"

Soleil Moon Fry (of *Punky Brewster* fame) says she is "a complete *Friends* freak". And it was a guest appearance on *Friends* in The One with the Girl Who Hits Joey that brought her back to Los Angeles after she'd taken a year off from acting to study social psychology at the New School in New York. Soleil played Matt LeBlanc's annoying girlfriend, Katie, who punched him every time she got excited. "In the end, Jennifer Aniston and I get into a fight. I had bruises on my arm for a week. She was *strong*."

▲ Joey took to wearing extra padding to protect himself from his pugnacious new girlfriend in The One with the Girl Who Hits Joey.

Rachel may not have had a Hot Guy in **The One with Rachel's Inadvertent Kiss**, but she did have an interview with a certain Mr Zelner for a big job at Ralph Lauren. Things went reasonably well, but as she was leaving she got the impression that Mr Zelner expected her to kiss him good-bye as he leaned over to open the door. So she kissed him on the cheek – to his obvious mystification. She was positive she'd blown the job until she got a call for a second interview. Wait a minute, she thought, what if that guy was thinking, "Let's bring back the girl who kisses everybody?" By the time she was through steaming herself up, she'd decided that he expected to sleep with her. So she told him off the minute she stepped into his office. "I am not some

"Just because I kissed you," Rachel told poor Mr Zelner, "that doesn't give you the right to demand sex from me!" ▼

was sorry he had had to find out this way. Suddenly Ross went all mushy. His best friend and his sister ... together ... and in love. Oh man ... this was *great*!

Now that he lived directly across from the gang, Ross spent a lot of time perfecting his shark-attack routine, which he performed in front of the window. While watching him, Joey caught sight of a beautiful woman who appeared to live down the hall, but every time he tried to find her he ended up at the wrong apartment – usually Ross's. So he walked through all the building's halls calling "Hot Girl!" at the top of his voice. Ultimately, it was Ross who found Hot Girl first..

"I love working with actors. In the same way that there's a collaboration between David and me, or Kevin and the two of us, there's a collaboration between the writer and the actor. If it doesn't make sense to the actor, you've got to rewrite it. Just because it makes sense in your head and you can do it, doesn't mean it's going to happen on the stage. So you've got to find a way to either put it in their terms or to rewrite it so it makes sense to them so they can perform it. It's a very exciting process." – Marta Kauffman

Courteney Cox, Jennifer Aniston and Marta Kauffman go over script changes on the set of The One with Rachel's Inadvertent Kiss.

CENTRAL PERK

"The coffee house was the final set to be built for the pilot. We wanted a place that had a lot of charm and warmth. Of course, we were old enough to remember the prototypical coffee houses from the sixties, and then Kevin S. Bright shot several small places in New York and brought us the photos. Set designer Greg Grande then styled the interior of Central Perk into an exaggerated living room – with oversized Victorian furniture and whimsical art – to recreate the dramatic coffee house look that was popular in L.A. and New York at the time."
– John Schaffner, art director.

HOLLYWOOD COFFEE SERVICE, INC.
DBA JOE TO GO
(95-3055803)
10153 1/2 Riverside Dr., #336
Toluca Lake, CA 91602
(213) 664-7200 FAX (213) 664-1167

Invoice

DATE	9/23/97
INVOICE NO.	1094

BILL TO
Friends
Candice
Warner Brother's #24

P.O. NO.	TERMS	DUE DATE	EPISODE
	Due on receipt	9/23/97	

SERVICED	ITEM	DESCRIPTION	AMOUNT
9/23/97	Coffee Beans	Joe Blend	150.00
	Coffee Beans	Vanilla Nut	85.00
	Coffee Beans	Kenya AA	97.50
	Coffee Beans	Organic Peru & Mexico	45.00

Candy,
Could you Ch...
into this i...
We're still sho...
as open.
Thanks
...

Thank you for your business!!

CENTRAL PERK

Coffee House Drinks

SPECIALTY DRINKS
Cappucino
espresso
cafe au lait
swiss latte
mochachino

CENTRAL JOLT JAVA
N.Y. CLASSICO
URBAN TRIBE JAVA
MANHATTAN MOCHA
LONG ISLAND CREAM
EMPIRE ROAST
MS. LIBERTY BLEND

"We're very proud of James Michael Tyler, who plays Gunther," says former *Friends* writer/producer Michael Curtis, "because we picked him out of the extras in the background at the coffee house. We gave him a line and he killed with it. Then we gave him a bigger line and he killed with that. Now people are recognizing him on the street."

▲ It's the Non-Mod Squad out to fight big-time crime on a ride-along with Gary the Cop.

hussy who will sleep around to get a job," she said tartly. "Just because I kissed you doesn't give you the right to demand sex from me!" Amazingly, Mr Zelner let Rachel come back in for a third interview when she requested it – although he was careful to tell her it was being videotaped. She presented a good defence of her behaviour, and it was clear that she desperately wanted the job. Against his better judgement, Mr Zelner decided to give it to her. She was so excited that she wanted to hug him, but, of course, he vetoed that. She tried to shake hands with him instead, but ended up grabbing his crotch. .

In **The One with the Ride-along** Ross was preoccupied with the fact that Emily's wedding was rapidly approaching. The truth was that he hadn't really given up on her, nor, apparently, she on him

▲ Chandler flirted with Caitlin (played by Kristin Dattilo), the cute pizza-delivery girl in The One Where Ross Can't Flirt.

Ross can so flirt, and he's going to prove it by flirting with Phoebe.

4 March 1999 "We have this wonderful bond where I feel protected, loved and cared about and it's not bullshit," Jennifer Aniston told Rolling Stone. "It's fun to watch people grow."

because she rang him and left a long message on his answering machine. "I'm getting married tomorrow," she began. "Or maybe I am. I keep thinking about you and wondering if we made a mistake by giving up so fast." But Emily's message went not to Ross, but to Rachel – who happened to be in his apartment borrowing ingredients for margaritas. What should she do? If Ross heard it, he might well get caught up in

◄ Phoebe had the bright idea of having the commitment-phobic Chandler try to talk Gary the Cop out of living with her.

Is this an episode of Murder on the Friends Express? No, the guys weren't trying to do away with Rachel, but, rather, to put drops in her eye as the doctor ordered to get rid of an annoying infection. ▼

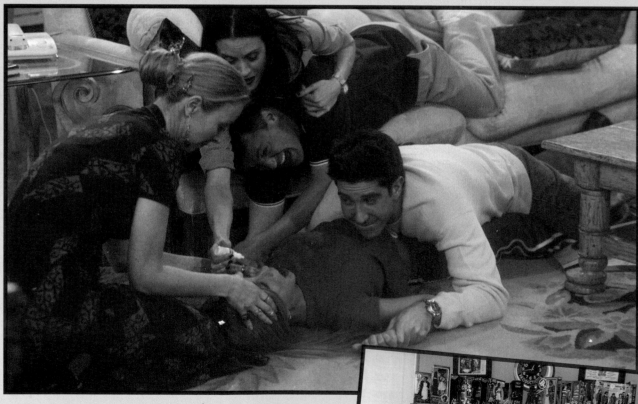

"There was a runner that went through the fifth year – references to Phoebe's having been in prison, which she drops every now and then. Like, she once said something about stabbing someone ... and her boyfriend, Gary the Cop, mentioned that he'd looked up her "record". It really catches you off guard to have this dark side come out of Phoebe, whom you think of as the flower child and the spiritual one of the group. I have a feeling we'll be finding out more about all that next year." – Kevin S. Bright

The Pop Kulture Klutter in executive producer Kevin S. Bright's office.

Joey: "Is this movie gonna be my big break?"
Chandler: "No. I mean yes."
— Joey heads out to Vegas for a lead role he landed.

Emily-madness again. But she couldn't just erase it ... could she? She dragged Monica over to help her decide

While Rachel and Monica pondered the moral implications of tampering with someone else's answering machine, Ross was out with Joey and Chandler in a squad-car ride-along with Phoebe's new boyfriend, Gary the Cop. Excited and a little scared, the guys thought they were being shot at when a car backfired. Courageously, Joey threw his body over Ross. Of course, Ross couldn't stop himself tearing up with gratitude – until Joey told him to cut it out or he'd kick his ass. Chandler, on the other hand, was clearly hurt by Joey's lack of concern about him. What was *he* ... chopped liver? Wasn't he supposed to be his best friend? If Chandler was going to be such a big baby, Joey would have to tell him what really went down. He was no hero ... he was just trying to save his incredibly delicious meatball sandwich, which had fallen on the other side of Ross's lap.

> "They can get married, and they can have children. They can do all of that as long as the six of them remain together as a unit."
> – Marta Kauffman

In the first version of the story that Ross told Rachel later, the car backfire had morphed back into a gun shot. OK, he back-pedalled, maybe it was only a backfire, but the incident had brought his life into stark relief. It was a message that he should stop obsessing over all the calamities of the past few months and get on with his life. If he really felt that way, Rachel responded, she had something to tell him. Emily had rung to say that she was having second thoughts about her wedding. Ross decided to take Emily's call as yet another sign – one that might mean that they were supposed to try again. But Rachel convinced him that all these many, many signs pointed to "escape". He'd *escaped* death – and now he should *escape* Emily.

By **The One with the Ball**, Gary had told Monica that he was going to ask Phoebe to move in with him. But Phoebe thought it was too soon for that kind of

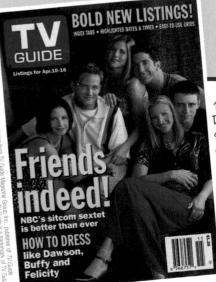

TV GUIDE
Listings for Apr.10-16
BOLD NEW LISTINGS!
INDEX TABS • HIGHLIGHTED DATES & TIMES • EASY-TO-USE GRIDS
Friends indeed!
NBC's sitcom sextet is better than ever
HOW TO DRESS like Dawson, Buffy and Felicity

10 April 1999 David Schwimmer said in the spring of 1999, "All I really want is to be treated like a regular person, though I realise sometimes that's impossible."

Mary Rodriguez (production coordinator), Todd Stevens (producer) and Jamie O'Connor (associate producer) compare notes. The trio have been with Friends since the pilot.

181

"Check me out ... I'm naked!" — Rachel

commitment. Why couldn't Gary be commitment-phobic like Chandler? That was a thought ... why not have Chandler talk Gary out of the whole moving-in-together thing? After all, he was an expert. "Are you crazy?" Chandler said to Gary later. "If you live with Phoebe, she's always gonna be there." Gary replied that that was fine with him. Chandler didn't get it. There was something wrong here. "Were your parents happy or something?" he asked. "Guilty," Gary responded, but more important than that, he was really in love. "You are worthless!" Phoebe yelled at Chandler.

In **The One with Joey's Big Break**, Joey had finally won a lead in a film. The movie was called *Shutter Speed,* and it was kind of a mystery-thriller thing. It was going to be shot in the desert outside Las Vegas, Joey told Chandler excitedly. And that could mean only one thing ... road trip! All they had to do was rent a car, but that reminded Phoebe that her grandmother was dead. That meant they

June 1999
"I went to a nutritionist," Jennifer Aniston says of her much-written-about body reconfiguration in the early Nineties. "She nearly threw me out of her office. I was eating mayonnaise sandwiches, fried foods, burgers. So I started to eat healthy and work out. I mean, I had never done anything."

▼ "Oh my god, that's Rachel naked!" – Ross

The guys were rolling out of town on the George Washington Bridge a few days later when Chandler admitted that he didn't think the movie was going to be Joey's big break. "What are you talking about?" Joey yelled. "I'm the lead in the movie!" "You're not even getting paid!" Chandler yelled back – although this was not an argument he particularly wanted to win. After a heated argument, Joey dropped Chandler off in the middle of rush-hour traffic.

Monica had bought Chandler something for their one-year anniversary that she was sure would cheer him up about the Joey fiasco (in **The One in Vegas, Parts I & II**): two aeroplane tickets to Las Vegas for the weekend! But as sweet as Monica's present was, Chandler was worried that Joey was going to be put out if they showed up there. No way, Monica assured him, he just didn't want them to go to any trouble. In that case, Phoebe was going, too, she chimed in eagerly. Chandler told her that they kind of wanted to be alone, seeing as it was their anniversary and all. "Oh no," she said, "you're not going to ditch me like you did with London." And then she proceeded to invite Ross and Rachel along as well.

could drive her cab cross country and save themselves some money. Which was a good thing, because Joey's film was a very low-budget affair, and as it was he was going to have to mooch a bed in Chandler's hotel room in order to afford the trip. "But once you get your first paycheque, you'll be swinging for a big hotel suite, right?" Chandler asked. "You're the lead … they must be paying you a lot." Not right now, Joey answered, but that didn't mean he didn't have a helluva deal: for every dollar *Shutter Speed* made, Joey told them proudly, he got one whole penny.

Rachel and Ross both had commitments that kept them from leaving New York until a day after the others. Rachel decided to follow Phoebe's advice and spend the night by herself being naked in the apartment. But, across the way, Ross could see her from his window, and he was pretty excited about her being naked, too.

"What Kevin does in the editing room is so astonishing," says producer Marta Kauffman. "We'll see a cut of the show and say, 'Oh God, this is terrible,' and he'll take it away, and I don't know what kind of spells he passes over it, but it will come back and it's hilarious." Here Kevin S. Bright and editor Steve Prime put the finishing touches on The One in Vegas, Part II.

The stash of nutritional health food snacks that keeps the Friends writers going through those grueling all-night sessions.

He realized that it wasn't right for him to be invading her privacy that way ... that is, unless she *wanted* him to look at her.

Rachel had to put on her bathrobe before she opened the door when Ross knocked a few minutes later. Ross launched straight into a speech about a no-strings-attached night based around the "physical act of love". Rachel asked him if he was out of his mind. "Then you weren't trying to entice me with your nakedness?" he asked weakly. Rachel tried not to laugh. "You actually thought I wanted to have sex with you?" she asked incredulously. "Of course not", he said in a very small voice.

Things weren't exactly perfect with Chandler and Monica, either – not after he found out that she had had lunch with her old flame, Richard. It wasn't just that she'd been with the hunky moustache-man, but that she'd lied about it. She promised she would tell him the next time she saw Richard. Fine, Chandler said, but that would have to be never. She didn't like him like this – all controlling and dictatorial. He didn't like him like this either, but that didn't mean he could stop. They agreed they would just as soon not be around each other, and headed off in opposite directions. Happy anniversary.

Ross and Rachel spent their flight to Las Vegas bickering and playing little pranks on each other – like Ross drawing a moustache on her face while she slept. A moustache that wouldn't wash off, it turned out. She refused to go out because people pointed and laughed at her, so Ross had to spend the rest of the night keeping her company in her hotel room. But it wasn't so bad: they played cards and drank all the little bottles of booze in the room fridge. Before long, they were totally plastered and Ross was ready for some action. Rachel said she would go downstairs with him, but only on one condition – that he let her draw cute little doodles on his face, too.

What...and give up show business? They stand in for the stars till the day comes when they get their own big break.

Make-up artist Beth Katz touches up Courteney Cox.

Monica was on her way up to the room to apologize to Chandler when she placed a bet at the crap table with a chip she'd found on the floor and ended up on a wild winning streak. Meanwhile, Phoebe interceded on her behalf with Chandler, telling him Monica loved *him*, not Richard. Joyfully convinced, he went down to join her as she rolled one winning combo after another. Finally he told her that if she rolled a hard eight, they would get married. One of the dice landed on a corner, but Chandler decided it was close enough. And they headed off to one of those quickie Vegas marriage marts. They sat down to wait outside the chapel, only to see the doors swing open and a super-sloshed Ross and Rachel career into the lobby. "Well helloooo, Mrs Ross!", he said to her with mock grandiosity. "Well helloooo, Mr Rachel!" she roared back. And then they staggered out into the night (in opposite directions) to throw up.

▲ Chandler: "I was there. I know Richard was the love of your life."
Monica: "Not any more ..."

►
Chandler told Monica that they would get married if she rolled a "hard eight".

Edward St George (hair) and Robin Siegel (make-up) buff Lisa Kudrow to a polished brilliance on the set of The One in Vegas.

We're Number One! Entertainment Weekly celebrates Friends' top-rated sitcom status in a July 1999 cover story.

THE
EPISODE
GUIDE

SEASON #1

THE PILOT
Written By: Marta Kauffman & David Crane
Directed By: James Burrows

T.O.W.T. Sonogram
Written By: Marta Kauffman & David Crane
Directed By: James Burrows

T.O.W.T. Thumb
Written By: Jeffrey Astrof & Mike Sikowitz
Directed By: James Burrows

T.O.W. George Stephanopoulos
Written By: Alexa Junge
Directed By: James Burrows

T.O.W.T. East German Laundry Detergent
Written By: Jeff Greenstein & Jeff Strauss
Directed By: Pamela Fryman

T.O.W.T. Butt
Written By: Adam Chase & Ira Ungerleider
Directed By: Arlene Sanford

T.O.W.T. Blackout
Written By: Jeffrey Astrof & Mike Sikowitz
Directed By: James Burrows

T.O. Where Nana Dies Twice
Written By: Marta Kauffman & David Crane
Directed By: James Burrows

T.O. Where Underdog Gets Away
Written By: Jeff Greenstein & Jeff Strauss
Directed By: James Burrows

T.O.W.T. Monkey
Written By: Adam Chase & Ira Ungerleider
Directed By: Peter Bonerz

T.O.W. Mrs. Bing
Written By: Alexa Junge
Directed By: James Burrows

T.O.W.T. Dozen Lasagnas
Written By: Jeffrey Astrof & Mike Sikowitz
Directed By: Paul Lazarus

T.O.W.T. Boobies
Written By: Alexa Junge
Directed By: Alan Myerson

T.O.W.T. Candy Hearts
Written By: Bill Lawrence
Directed By: James Burrows

T.O.W.T. Stoned Guy
Written By: Jeff Greenstein & Jeff Strauss
Directed By: Alan Myerson

T.O.W. Two Parts Part 1
Written By: Marta Kauffman & David Crane
Directed By: Michael Lembeck

T.O.W. Two Parts Part 2
Written By: Marta Kauffman & David Crane
Directed By: Michael Lembeck

T.O.W. All The Poker
Written By: Jeffrey Astrof & Mike Sikowitz
Directed By: James Burrows

T.O. Where The Monkey Gets Away
Written By: Jeffrey Astrof & Mike Sikowitz
Directed By: Peter Bonerz

T.O.W.T. Evil Orthodontist
Written By: Doty Abrams
Directed By: Peter Bonerz

T.O.W.T. Fake Monica
Written By: Adam Chase & Ira Ungerleider
Directed By: Gail Mancuso

T.O.W.T. Ick Factor
Written By: Alexa Junge
Directed By: Robby Benson

T.O.W.T. Birth
Written By: Marta Kauffman & David Crane
Directed By: James Burrows

T.O. Where Rachel Finds Out
Written By: Chris Brown
Directed By: Kevin S. Bright

SEASON 1 CREDITS

Executive Producers	Kevin S. Bright
	Marta Kauffman
	David Crane
Supervising Producers	Jeff Greenstein
	Jeff Strauss
Produced By	Todd Stevens
Story Editors	Ira Ungerleider
	Adam Chase
	Alexa Junge
	Jeff Astrof
	Mike Sikowitz
Staff Writers	Bill Lawrence
	Jenji Cohen

SEASON #2

T.O.W. Ross's New Girlfriend
Written By: Jeffrey Astrof & Mike Sikowitz
Directed By: Michael Lembeck

T.O.W.T. Breast Milk
Written By: Adam Chase & Ira Underleider
Directed By: Michael Lembeck

T.O. Where Heckles Dies
Written By: Michael Curtis & Gregory S. Malins
Directed By: Kevin S. Bright

T.O.W. Phoebe's Husband
Written By: Alexa Junge
Directed By: Gail Mancuso

T.O.W. Five Steaks & An Eggplant
Written By: Chris Brown
Directed By: Ellen Gittelsohn

T.O.W.T Baby On The Bus
Written By: Betsy Borns
Directed By: Gail Mancuso

T.O. Where Ross Finds Out
Written By: Michael Borkow
Directed By: Peter Bonerz

T.O.W.T. List
Written By: Marta Kauffman & David Crane
Directed By: Mary Kay Place

T.O.W. Phoebe's Dad
Written By: Jeffrey Astrof & Mike Sikowitz
Directed By: Kevin S. Bright

T.O.W. Russ
Written By: Ira Ungerleider
Directed By: Thomas Schlamme

T.O.W.T. Lesbian Wedding
Written By: Doty Abrams
Directed By: Thomas Schlamme

T.O. After The Super Bowl Part 1
Written By: Jeffrey Astrof & Mike Sikowitz
Directed By: Michael Lembeck

T.O. After The Super Bowl Part 2
Written By: Michael Borkow
Directed By: Michael Lembeck

T.O.W.T. Prom Video
Written By: Alexa Junge
Directed By: James Burrows

T.O.W. Ross & Rachel...You Know
Written By: Michael Curtis & Gregory S. Malins
Directed By: Michael Lembeck

T.O. Where Joey Moves Out
Written By: Betsy Borns
Directed By: Michael Lembeck

T.O. Where Eddie Moves In
Written By: Adam Chase
Directed By: Michael Lembeck

T.O. Where Dr. Ramoray Dies
Written By: Alexa Junge
Directed By: Michael Lembeck

T.O. Where Eddie Won't Go
Written By: Michael Curtis & Gregory S. Malins
Directed By: Michael Lembeck

T.O. Where Old Yeller Dies
Written By: Michael Curtis & Gregory S. Malins
Directed By: Michael Lembeck

T.O.W.T. Bullies
Written By: Sebastian Jones & Brian Buckner
Directed By: Michael Lembeck

T.O.W.T. Chicken Pox
Written By: Brown Mandel
Directed By: Michael Lembeck

T.O.W. Barry & Mindy's Wedding
Written By: Ira Ungerleider
Teleplay By: Brown Mandel
Directed By: Michael Lembeck

CREDITS SEASON #2
Executive Producers ....Kevin S. Bright
....Marta Kauffman
....David Crane
Supervising Producer ....Michael Borkow
Produced By...Todd Stevens
Producer...Betsy Borns
Executive Story Editors...........................Ira Ungerleider
....Adam Chase
....Alexa Junge
....Jeff Astrof
....Mike Sikowitz
....Michael Curtis
....Gregory S. Malins

SEASON #3

T.O.W.T. Princess Leia Fantasy
Written By: Michael Curtis & Gregory S. Malins
Directed By: Gail Mancuso

T.O. Where No One's Ready
Written By: Ira Ungerleider
Directed By: Gail Mancuso

T.O.W.T. Jam
Written By: Will Calhoun
Directed By: Kevin S. Bright

T.O.W.T. Metaphorical Tunnel
Written By: Alexa Junge
Directed By: Steve Zuckerman

T.O.W. Frank Jr
Written By: Scott Silveri & Shana Goldberg-Meehan
Directed By: Steve Zuckerman

T.O.W.T. Flashback
Written By: Marta Kauffman & David Crane
Directed By: Peter Bonerz

T.O.W.T. Race Car Bed
Written By: Seth Kurland
Directed By: Gail Mancuso

T.O.W.T. Giant Poking Device
Written By: Adam Chase
Directed By: Gail Mancuso

T.O.W.T. Football
Written By: Ira Ungerleider
Directed By: Kevin S. Bright

T.O. Where Rachel Quits
Written By: Michael Curtis & Gregory S. Malins
Directed By: Terry Hughes

T.O. Where Chandler Can't Remember
Written By: Alexa Junge
Directed By: Terry Hughes

T.O.W. All The Jealousy
Written By: Doty Abrams
Directed By: Robby Benson

T.O. Where Monica & Richard Are Just Friends
Written By: Michael Borkow
Directed By: Robby Benson

T.O.W. Phoebe's Ex-Partner
Written By: Wil Calhoun
Directed By: Robby Benson

T.O. Where Ross & Rachel Take A Break
Written By: Michael Borkow
Directed By: James Burrows

T.O.T. Morning After
Written By: Marta Kauffman & David Crane
Directed By: James Burrows

T.O. Without The Ski Trip
Written By: Scott Silveri & Shana Goldberg-Meehan
Directed By: Sam Simon

T.O.W.T. Hypnosis Tape
Written By: Seth Kurland
Directed By: Robby Benson

T.O.W.T. Tiny T-Shirt
Written By: Adam Chase
Directed By: Terry Hughes

T.O.W.T. Dollhouse
Written By: Wil Calhoun
Directed By: Terry Hughes

T.O.W.T. Chick And A Duck
Written By: Chris Brown
Directed By: Michael Lembeck

T.O.W.T. Screamer
Written By: Scott Silveri & Shana Goldberg-Meehan
Directed By: Peter Bonerz

T.O.W. Ross's Thing
Written By: Andrew Reich & Ted Cohen
Directed By: Shelley Jensen

T.O.W.T. Ultimate Fighting Champion
Written By: Mark J. Kunerth & Pang-ni Landrum
Teleplay By: Scott Silveri & Shana Goldberg-Meehan
Directed By: Robby Benson

T.O. At The Beach
Teleplay By: Adam Chase
Story By: Pang-ni Landrum & Mark J. Kunerth
Directed By: Pamela Fryman

SEASON #3 CREDITS

Executive Producers	Kevin S. Bright
	Marta Kauffman
	David Crane
Co-Executive Producer	Michael Borkow
Produced By	Todd Stevens
Producers	Adam Chase
	Michael Curtis
	Gregory S. Malins
	Alexa Junge
	Ira Ungerleider
Creative Consultant	Richard Rosenstock
Executive Story Editors	Wil Calhoun
	Seth Kurland
	Shana Goldberg-Meehan
	Scott Silveri

SEASON #4

T.O.W.T. Jellyfish
Written By: Wil Calhoun
Directed By: Shelley Jenson

T.O.W.T. Cat
Written By: Jill Condon & Amy Toomin
Directed By: Shelley Jenson

T.O.W.T. Cuffs
Written By: Seth Kurland
Directed By: Peter Bonerz

T.O.W.T. Ballroom Dancing
Written By: Andrew Reich & Ted Cohen
Directed By: Gail Mancuso

T.O.W. Joey's New Girlfriend
Written By: Michael Curtis & Gregory S. Malins
Directed By: Gail Mancuso

T.O.W.T. Dirty Girl
Written By: Scott Silveri & Shana Goldberg-Meehan
Directed By: Shelley Jenson

T.O. Where Chandler Crosses The Line
Written By: Adam Chase
Directed By: Kevin S. Bright

T.O.W. Chandler In A Box
Written By: Michael Borkow
Directed By: Peter Bonerz

T.O. Where They're Going To Party
Written By: Andrew Reich & Ted Cohen
Directed By: Peter Bonerz

T.O.W.T. Girl From Poughkeepsie
Written By: Scott Silveri
Directed By: Gary Halverson

T.O.W. Phoebe's Uterus
Written By: Seth Kurland
Directed By: David Steinberg

T.O.W.T. Embryos
Written By: Jill Condon & Amy Toomin
Directed By: Kevin S. Bright

T.O.W. Rachel's Crush
Written By: Shana Goldberg-Meehan
Directed By: Dana J. deVally

T.O.W. Joey's Dirty Day
Written By: Wil Calhoun
Directed By: Peter Bonerz

T.O.W. All The Rugby
Written By: Andrew Reich & Ted Cohen
Directed By: James Burrows

T.O.W.T. Fake Party
Story By: Alicia Sky Varinaitis
Teleplay By: Shana Goldberg-Meehan & Scott Silveri
Directed By: Michael Lembeck

T.O.W.T. Free Porn
Story By: Mark J. Kunerth
Teleplay By: Richard Goodman
Directed By: Michael Lembeck

T.O.W. Rachel's New Dress
Story By: Andrew Reich & Ted Cohen
Teleplay By: Jill Condon & Amy Toomin
Directed By: Gail Mancuso

T.O.W. All The Haste
Written By: Wil Calhoun & Scott Silveri
Directed By: Kevin S. Bright

T.O.W. All The Wedding Dresses
Story By: Adam Chase
Teleplay By: Michael Curtis & Gregory S. Malins
Directed By: Gail Mancuso

T.O.W.T. Invitation
Written By: Seth Kurland
Directed By: Peter Bonerz

T.O.W.T. Worst Best Man Ever
Story By: Seth Kurland
Teleplay By: Michael Curtis & Gregory S. Malins
Directed By: Peter Bonerz

T.O.W. Ross's Wedding Part 1
Written By: Michael Borkow
Directed By: Kevin S. Bright

T.O.W. Ross's Wedding Part 2
Story By: Jill Condon & Amy Toomin
Teleplay By: Shana Goldberg-Meehan & Scott Silveri
Directed By: Kevin S. Bright

SEASON #4 CREDITS

Executive Producers ....Kevin S. Bright
....Marta Kauffman
....David Crane
Executive Producer ....Michael Borkow
Co-Executive Producers ....Adam Chase
....Michael Curtis
....Gregory S. Malins
Produced By ....Todd Stevens
Co-Producers ....Wil Calhoun
....Seth Kurland
....Jill Condon
....Amy Toomin
Executive Story Editors ....Shana Goldberg-Meehan
....Scott Silveri
....Andrew Reich
....Ted Cohen

SEASON #5

T.O. After Ross Says Rachel
Written By: Seth Kurland
Directed By: Kevin S. Bright

T.O.W. All The Kissing
Written By: Wil Carhoun
Directed By: Gary Halverson

T. One Hundredth
Written By: Marta Kauffman & David Crane
Directed By: Kevin S. Bright

T.O. Where Phoebe Hates PBS
Written By: Michael Curtis
Directed By: Shelley Jensen

T.O.W. All The Kips
Written By: Scott Silveri
Directed By: Dana deVally

T.O.W.T. Yeti
Written By: Alexa Junge
Directed By: Gary Halverson

T.O. Where Ross Moves In
Written By: Perry Rein & Gigi McCreery
Directed By: Gary Halverson

T.O.W. All The Thanksgivings
Written By: Gregory S. Malins
Directed By: Kevin S. Bright

T.O.W. Ross's Sandwich
Written By: Andrew Reich & Ted Cohen
Directed By: Gary Halverson

T.O.W.T. Inappropriate Sister
Written By: Shana Goldberg-Meehan
Directed By: Dana deVally Piazza

T.O.W. All The Resolutions
Story By: Brian Boyle
Teleplay By: Suzie Villandry
Directed By: Joe Regalbuto

T.O.W. Chandler's Work Laugh
Written By: Alicia Sky Varinaitis
Directed By: Kevin S. Bright

T.O.W. Joey's Bag
Written By: Seth Kurland
Directed By: Gail Mancuso

T.O.W. Everybody Finds Out
Written By: Alexa Junge
Directed By: Michael Lembeck

T.O.W.T. Girl Who Hits Joey
Written By: Adam Chase
Directed By: Kevin S. Bright

T.O.W.T. Cop
Story By: Alicia Sky Varinaitis
Teleplay By: Gigi McCreery & Perry Rein
Directed By: Andrew Tsao

T.O.W. Rachel's Inadvertent Kiss
Written By: Andrew Reich & Ted Cohen
Directed By: Shelley Jensen

T.O. Where Rachel Smokes
Written By: Michael Curtis
Directed By: Todd Holland

T.O.W. Ross Can't Flirt
Written By: Doty Abrams
Directed By: Gail Mancuso

T.O.W.T. Ride-Along
Written By: Shana Goldberg-Meehan & Seth Kurland
Directed By: Gary Halverson

T.O.W.T. Ball
Teleplay By: Gregory S. Malins
Story By: Scott Silveri
Directed By: Gary Halverson

T.O.W. Joey's Big Break
Teleplay By: Wil Calhoun
Story By: Shana Goldberg-Meehan
Directed By: Gary Halverson

T.O. In Vegas Part 1
Written By: Andrew Reich & Ted Cohen
Directed By: Kevin S. Bright

T.O. In Vegas Part 2
Written By: Gregory S. Malins & Scott Silveri
Directed By: Kevin S. Bright

SEASON #5 CREDITS

Executive Producers	Kevin S. Bright
	Marta Kauffman
	David Crane
	Adam Chase
	Michael Curtis
	Gregory S. Malins
Co-Executive Producer	Alexa Junge
Supervising Producers	Todd Stevens
	Wil Calhoun
	Seth Kurland
Producers	Shana Goldberg-Meehan
	Scott Silveri
Co-Producers	Andrew Reich
	Ted Cohen
	Wendy Knoller
Executive Story Editors	Gigi McCreery
	Perry Rein

PHOEBE'S SONGS

Composition: "Smelly Cat"
Original Title: same as above
Writers: Lisa Kudrow, Betsy Borns, Adam Chase
Copyright date: 1995
Publisher(s): Warner-Tamerlane Publishing Corp. (BMI).
WB Music Corp. (ASCAP)

Composition: "Two of Them Kissed (Last Night)"
Original Title: "He Must Decide"
Writers: Lisa Kudrow, Marta Kauffman, David Crane
Copyright Date: 1995
Publisher(s): Warner-Tamerlane Publishing Corp. (BMI).
WB Music Corp. (ASCAP)

Composition: "Don't"
Original Title: "That's Another Thing You Don't Want To Do"
Writers: Lisa Kudrow, Jeff Astrof, Mike Sikowitz
Copyright Date: 1996
Publisher(s): Warner-Tamerlane Publishing Corp. (BMI)

Composition: "Terry's A Jerk"
Original Title: same as above
Writers: Lisa Kudrow, Betsy Borns
Copyright Date: 1995
Publisher(s): Warner-Tamerlane Publishing Corp. (BMI)

Composition: "The Book of Love"
Original Title: "Sometimes"
Writers: Lisa Kudrow, Jeff Astrof, Mike Sikowitz
Copyright Date: 1996
Publisher(s): Warner-Tamerlane Publishing Corp. (BMI)

Composition: "The Animal Song"
Original Title: "Oh, The Cow in the Meadow Goes Moo"
Writers: Lisa Kudrow, Jeff Astrof, Mike Sikowitz
Copyright Date: 1996
Publisher(s): Warner-Tamerlane Publishing Corp. (BMI)

Composition: "The Snowman"
Original Title: "Dead Mother Song #1"
Writers: Lisa Kudrow, Adam Chase, Ira Ungerleider
Copyright Date: 1994
Publisher(s): Warner-Tamerlane Publishing Corp. (BMI).
WB Music Corp. (ASCAP)

Composition: "Mother's Ashes"
Original Title: "Dead Mother Song #2"
Writers: Lisa Kudrow, Adam Chase, Ira Ungerleider
Copyright Date: 1994
Publisher(s): Warner-Tamerlane Publishing Corp. (BMI).
WB Music Corp. (ASCAP)

Composition: "Blackout"
Original Title: "New York City Has No Power"
Writers: Lisa Kudrow, Lynn Mandell
Copyright Date: 1994
Publisher(s): Warner-Tamerlane Publishing. (BMI)

Composition: "Love Song"
Original Title: "Coma Guy Song"
Writers: Lisa Kudrow, Alexa Junge
Copyright Date: 1995
Publisher(s): Warner-Tamerlane Publishing Corp. (BMI).
WB Music Corp. (ASCAP)

Composition: "Shower Song"
Original Title: "I'm in the Shower"
Writers: Lisa Kudrow, Betsy Borns
Copyright Date: 1995
Publisher(s): Warner-Tamerlane Publishing Corp. (BMI)